DON'T WALK IN THE LONG GRASS

DON'T WALK
IN THE
LONG GRASS

Tenniel Evans

BANTAM PRESS

LONDON · NEW YORK · TORONTO · SYDNEY · AUCKLAND

TRANSWORLD PUBLISHERS LTD
61–63 Uxbridge Road, London W5 5SA

TRANSWORLD PUBLISHERS (AUSTRALIA) PTY LTD
15–25 Helles Avenue, Moorebank, NSW 2170

TRANSWORLD PUBLISHERS (NZ) LTD
3 William Pickering Drive, Albany, Auckland

Published 1999 by Bantam Press
a division of Transworld Publishers Ltd
Copyright © by Tenniel Evans 1999

A catalogue record for this book is available from the British Library.

ISBN 0593 043812

Typeset in 11 on 14 pt Goudy by
Hewer Text Ltd, Edinburgh

Printed in Great Britain by Clays Ltd, Bungay, Suffolk

*For Evangeline
and in memory of my parents and
of Alison and Rupert Winser*

INTRODUCTION
by Alec Guinness

T HE TITLE IS THE CONSTANT INJUNCTION, REPEATED LIKE A mantra, to Tenniel Evans and his brother and sisters by their mother when they were children in Kenya. As a small boy he ran barefoot around his parents' ramshackle farm in what sounds a foolhardy way; there were spiky and poisonous things underfoot, a green mamba lurking in a tree (until misfired at by the resourceful and intrepid Mrs Evans, when it disappeared in a flash, leaving one or two of the locals in a dead faint), an alarming great feral cat and, never far distant, hyenas and the roar of a lion. The family seems to have been close-knit and happy except for the financial disasters which periodically overtook them. Mr Evans, an Old Etonian of great charm, tackled each new crazy enterprise he thought up with rash enthusiasm, and every one of them was doomed to spectacular failure.

This book is a delightful, swift and easy read; always vivid, very often funny and sometimes exciting. You get a clear and loving view of Kenya through the alert eyes and ears of an eight-year-old boy. The same awareness is there when he is sent on his own to England to start his proper schooling. He had gained a scholarship to the Blue Coats. (I am about a dozen years older than Tenniel Evans and I well remember, when going back to my own school, always seeing Blue Coat boys on a platform at Victoria Station. I envied them their smart Elizabethan uniform of a long dark blue surcoat with a leather belt and canary yellow stockings showing from above the ankles; it seemed to me an admirable get-up for any aspiring actor.) Arriving in a chilly London with only light-weight tropical clothes he was met at the docks by a kindly aunt who whisked him off to one of the larger stores where he was kitted out. He was tremendously proud of a pair of woollen gloves, never having worn gloves before, but soon found, as I had done a decade before, that although they were fine for keeping hands warm they were useless, fumbling things when it came to doing up buttons and so on. Also, I suspect they produced chilblains.

His accounts of his English relatives are full of loving appreciation. He takes his juvenile tale to the end of school days and we must hope he will continue with another volume detailing his early experiences in the theatre. I have never met him but I have seen distinguished performances he has given. His reputation as a man I do know; everyone who has worked with him smiles happily when his name is mentioned and speaks of his good humour and Christian kindness. Not long ago I heard a story about him which I hope is not apocryphal. He was playing one of the King's minions, either Bushy, Bagot or Green, in a production of *Richard II*; at the dress rehearsal

2

the three of them gazed at each other in their over-the-top camp costumes with a wild surmise. 'Do you think,' asked Tenniel Evans, 'we look as if we are a threat to the Plantagenets?'

I

MY AUNT EDIE LIT ANOTHER CIGARETTE AND INHALED deeply. 'We're not going to Leamington,' she said.

The train wheels went clickety-clack, clickety-clack. There was just enough light to see black silhouettes of trees and houses gliding past the window. I had been lulled into a kind of doze. It had been a long day.

I looked at her uncomprehendingly. Leamington had been, for as long as I could remember, what the word 'England' represented; Leamington had been my destination from the moment I had said a tear-drenched farewell to my mother and father on Kisumu station over a month before; Leamington, as far as I was concerned, was the only town in England.

Aunt Edith had collected me off the *Dunluce Castle* in the London docks that morning and we had become friends. She showed me Westminster Hall, and reclothed me in warm winter gear at D. H. Evans, to replace the light tropical outfit and broad-brimmed terai hat in which I had shivered as I waited on deck for her. I was particularly proud of my woollen gloves. I had never worn gloves before; they were, I felt, a mark of distinction. She had fed me whiting with their tails in their mouths afterwards in the busy shop restaurant, and we had caught a cab to smelly Euston and boarded this important-sounding train.

'Auntie Duff', my father's younger sister, was a plump little woman in her forties. I suppose she was 'plain', for she had thin straight hair cut short for convenience, prominent watery-blue eyes, a little button of a nose which shone in the cold, and a ready smile more gum than teeth. But I already loved her, and knew an inner beauty which was all I ever saw. As soon as she had scooped me off that ship, I had at least one friend in this noisy, frosty England. Duff was unmarried and lived with her elder sister Norah in York Road, Leamington Spa. And Leamington was my haven, the port in which I could finally rest after my long and bewildering journey.

Now she was saying that I was not going to Leamington at all.

It must have been a difficult moment for her. I was stricken and could only stare. She dealt with it manfully.

'No – we're actually going to Coventry' – I had never heard of Coventry – 'and you're going to live with Cousin Ailie.' She grinned bravely. 'You'll be much happier there.'

'Why?' It was all I could think of saying.

'Well, your Aunt Norah's not too well, and Mrs Town-send's getting on—' Mrs Townsend was a legend. Her name held the promise of cushions and a warm kitchen. How could she be 'getting on'?

Duff took some quick puffs at her cigarette. 'And the house

is really very small . . .' Her voice faltered as she looked at my face. 'You'll love Ailie – she's great fun – and she has four children.'

Four children. I had never enjoyed the company of other people's 'children'. I looked at her forlornly.

'I hope this journey goes on for ever,' I said.

But the train to Coventry clattered remorselessly on.

It stopped, I remember, at a station called Brandon and Wolston. There was a lot of hissing steam and porters calling 'BRAAAND'N'WOLSTERN', and a great uncompanionable argument of milk churns. Then the engine gave another huge puff and a lot of little ones, and we ground into movement again.

'Next stop is us,' said Duff, and took my hand. Life was banked up with threatening clouds.

The train clanked and swayed over a myriad of points; naked lights gleamed coldly through the misty darkness. People began to collect their bits of luggage. I looked at Duff. She smiled gummily and nodded. The brakes screeched as we slowed, and the lights of a station slid into view. A large board said COVENTRY. With two or three jerks the train pulled up, and passengers made impatiently for the door. An icy draught sidled in as it opened.

We were the last out and, as I stepped down onto the platform, I noticed opposite us the tall figure of a woman. She was wearing a firm wide-brimmed hat and a thick tweed overcoat with a fur collar, turned up against the cold.

She opened her coat and undid the inside tie which held it

together. She stepped towards me, and folded the coat around me. She had an odd dry smell. I did not know what the hell was going on.

'Hello, old man,' I heard her say. 'Welcome home!'

I heard many years later that, when my father's cousin Alison heard from Duff that I was on my way from Kenya, destined to live in Leamington with two maiden aunts who scarcely knew which end of a small boy was which, she had said very firmly, as was her wont: 'That child can't possibly live with you. You'd better give him to me.' And my fate was decided, without further ado. My dearest Duff must have heaved a huge sigh of relief. Mrs Townsend, her housekeeper, was indeed getting frail; Sam Townsend was in and out of hospital with 'his heart'; and Aunt Norah suffered badly from epileptic fits. It was no environment for a small boy from the tropics, or anywhere else. This strange-smelling woman, with a warm laugh and a hard, unyielding breast, was to become the centre of my life and give me the sound, middle-class upbringing that I could never have had among my own hand-to-mouth, tumbledown family, scrambling a precarious living on the fringes of Kenya society. Inevitably, I was to grow away from them, until we had little in common save reminiscences.

One of the popular misconceptions about life in the colonies was that the whites were all rich and lived a life of unbridled luxury. It was a useful political stick with which to beat the empire-builders and plutocrats and, like all simplifications, it was wide of the mark.

Of course, there were rich and prosperous settlers. They had managed to acquire the best bits of land when Kenya was first colonized and made a wonderful life for themselves. And it is part of history that there was a layer of spoiled, wealthy folk who had earned for Kenya the reputation of being a place in the sun for shady people. Popular authors before the war, when a character blotted his copybook or had become redundant to the plot, often packed him off to grow coffee or shoot lions in Kenya. We had all heard about the 'Happy Valley', the parties, the scandals, the elopements, suicides – even the occasional sensational murder.

But the great majority of white settlers worked very hard to make a living, and the risks and wantonness of a tropical climate kept them from making the kind of money with which popular legend has endowed them. Certainly, my family was much too poor, our life too close to the earth, for such legends to have any sort of reality. Compared with the Africans, to be sure, we were rich beyond the dreams of avarice – hard up though we were, we always managed to employ houseboys, *shamba*-boys who worked on the farm, men to drive the tractor and girls to clean the house. That was one of the attractions of having colonies.

But among Europeans such conditions were taken for granted: there was a certain standard below which it would occur to very few white people to fall. It was an ethnic, not a cultural, standard, like the colour bar: accepted without question by both black and white on the up-country farms and in the little townships which supplied them. It was unthinkable for the whites to live as the African did. Those who did – and there were a few – were not so much shunned as pitied, by both races. And the colour bar was hardly ever questioned. When it was, usually by the occasional missionary, it was thought of more as a mental aberration than a political threat. It simply was not a subject about which it was worth arguing. Before I went to school nearly all my friends were black, and I shared their life and their food, probably more than my parents would have approved of, had they known it all. To my black friends' parents I was just another *toto*. But I was white, and that made the difference; they would no more have been allowed in my home than were the dogs.

Nevertheless, as I said, by white standards my family came a long way down the pecking order; our contacts with the rich white world were few. This was just as well – we could never have afforded to keep up the pace. All the same, we believed that it was important to maintain the facade of white superiority; and, indeed, when the colour bar did become an issue, at the first stirrings of independence, it was those, like my family, who lived closest to the boundary line, who were the most rigid in maintaining it.

Of course, it was not until I came to England that I discovered an almost equally rigid class divide. Indeed, almost my first contact with my newly imposed family caused a ruffling of feathers.

After Aunt Ailie Winser had greeted us at Coventry, she led us outside the station where a smart new Morris 10 stood. It was a cold, raw November evening and I was glad to tumble into the back. My tin trunk had been sent off in advance from the docks, so we only had our hand luggage – consisting mainly of my discarded tropical gear – and I was grateful for my woolly gloves, though already I had found out how clumsy they made me.

'It's November twenty-fifth – did you know that, Edie?'

'Oh, my dear – it's your silver wedding – I'd completely forgotten,' said Duff in a tone I grew to know well in succeeding years.

I knew what a silver wedding was because we had had a gymkhana to celebrate the silver jubilee of King George V and Queen Mary. I thought it only applied to kings and queens.

'No, dear,' said Ailie. 'Twenty-one, not twenty-five.' So what was twenty-one?

We drove through the narrow, brightly lit streets and out onto the old Birmingham road. After a couple of miles the road narrowed between high banks and we turned right, up a steep little lane.

'Here we are,' said Ailie. (I still did not really know what she looked like; but I suddenly remembered my father's voice: 'Cousin Ailie. Good sport. Face just like a horse.') 'Allesley. We're home.'

We turned in at some gates which seemed to be embedded in great dark bushes.

The car crunched its way round a gravel drive and pulled up in front of an enormous ugly house which rose up into the dark night sky above. There were lights on everywhere, right up to the top. The house had a too-small porch, above which shone a naked bulb. I thought the place looked like a hotel.

Duff had explained rather hurriedly in the train that Aunt Ailie was my father's first cousin and was the wife of Rupert Winser who was the rector of Allesley. I did not know what a rector was, except that it had something to do with church. Whatever it meant, by the look of the house he didn't have a bad job.

We scrambled out of the car and I snatched a quick look at my father's cousin. He was right – she did look like a horse, with an amused expression in her eyes as if she were about to neigh. I decided I liked the look of her.

The porch door opened at that moment and a youth in a dinner jacket came out. He looked beautiful and healthy, with a lot of dark curly hair. Ailie introduced us.

'This is Bobby,' she said.

I had only ever seen a dinner jacket on the staff in the ship's dining room. I was very impressed.

'You look just like a steward,' I said admiringly; and understood neither the slight chill in the atmosphere nor Ailie's whoop of laughter.

Bobby gave me a fifteen-year-old's look, and Duff a kiss, as a tall, handsome, pink-faced clergyman with thinning grey hair came out to greet us. Uncle Rupert. The rector. He smiled benignly. 'Ah, my dears. How lovely!'

'Rupert,' said Duff, 'this is Walter . . .'

'Ah, yes – Galterus Evansus. Ave – welcome!' I did not

know what he was talking about. I was vaguely embarrassed and so was he.

We entered the house, which was dark and not very warm and full of strange smells. I was suddenly overcome with a great pang of homesickness. The clear, star-encompassed darkness of a Kenya night, with the smell of woodsmoke and dry grass, and the warmth of my own dear family, seemed so very far away. I did not dare to think about my mother. But I could see my father, tall and spare and upright; a military figure, with a clipped moustache and a light pith helmet at a jaunty angle, a thumb stuck into his belt.

Part of his charm was a resilience in the face of disaster and an apparently inexhaustible sense of humour at the persistently hopeless cards which fate seemed to deal him. I suspect, though, that the basis of this seeming strength was a lack of compassion and care for the fate of those who were dependent on him. Duff told me many years later that he was the scamp of his family as a boy, and could always charm his way out of trouble. Duff was his younger sister, Edith, and never spoke of him without an indulgent chuckle. Which was exactly how his consistent failure to make ends meet was greeted by our family. I do not think it ever occurred to any of us to blame him and, as far as I can tell, he went through his whole life with a blithe lack of self-reproach which I can only envy. My mother told me that, about a week before he died in 1950, she was watching him swimming in the sea at Nyali and, as his arm came up in a perfect crawl stroke, she saw that he was wearing her gold watch, one of her last family possessions from her childhood. She chuckled fondly as she told me.

But he was lovely. He made my mother happy. He made us laugh, and was the best storyteller I ever knew. He never disciplined us – he had no need to; my mother did that. He was a jolly Edwardian gentleman.

I worshipped my father. He was funny, fierce, attractive – and histrionic: when he was being sick during one of his frequent bouts of malaria, it was like the death throes of a dinosaur. We tiptoed round the house, wide-eyed and anxious, not daring to laugh at the outrageous noises he was making.

He was a wonderful storyteller and read to us from his favourite authors – Kipling, Edgar Wallace and Surtees. ' "What's the weather like, Jorrocks?" – to the red-faced huntsman who had put his drunken head into the larder instead of out the window – "Dark as hell, sir, and stinks abominably of cheese." '

He told us his favourite George Robey jokes. 'Diner, to waiter, having just bitten into an olive: "Waiter, Waiter. Somebody's peed on these plums." Old codger, on a bench, solemnly picking his teeth: " 'Am? 'Am? 'Aven't 'ad 'am for a fortnit." '

These stories were often repeated amid gales of infectious laughter. I laughed too, but I did not understand any of them.

Duff remembered her brother with adoration. Geoffrey was the handsome, indulged younger son of well-off parents. He could never hang on to money, but was always fun to be with, she said. Well, I knew that.

'Father's got a hole in his pocket,' my mother used to say. Someone had always fleeced him, my sisters claimed.

I had always wondered about this. Other people managed to hang on to their money, but not Father.

There was the story of the cattle. When I was a tiny baby – in fact, in 1926 – Father had managed to rear a fine herd of pedigree cattle, the pride of the district. He liked cattle; he had learnt about them in Australia, he told us. Leaving them in the care of my godfather's eldest son, he brought the family to England for a holiday (the last time Duff had seen me). When we returned to Kenya the beautiful cattle were no more; an epidemic of rinderpest had knocked them out. Or had it? The herd was not insured; the friend was a cheerful rogue, who somehow had cleared off all his debts while we were away; there was no sign of the incinerators. Father must have been diddled, the family said.

But they had said that about his father Walter when *he* went bust. The old man must have been quite rich once. He managed to send Father to Eton, where he became a Wet Bob (something to do with rowing). He owned a colliery outside Nuneaton. And lost it. Through no fault of his own, I was told.

This was why Father went overseas in the first place. He intended to go to South Africa, where he had served in the Boer War. But he fell in love with a girl on the boat, who was heading for Australia. He changed his plans at Cape Town,

14

sold his guns and fishing gear to pay for his ticket, and sailed on to Sydney with his beloved. He could tell us no more of the lady, because the moment they disembarked she ditched him.

He told us wonderful stories of the Australian gold rush – of prospectors coming into Brisbane full of tales of river beds gleaming yellow in the sun and paying for a suit of clothes with a bagful of gold dust. He sang us songs about gambling saloons running with booze and bedbugs, and knife fights in the street over women and gold.

He brought no gold from Australia, but he did bring something more precious: my mother Alice. She was the daughter of John Ashton King, a doctor from Ambleside who had emigrated to Brisbane with a large family. We never met them, but we knew they had names like Col and Vi and Meg and Doll, and they sent her eucalyptus seeds which she planted round the house at Porgies.

For Father had returned to England when the Great War broke out, and after it was over he escaped again, this time to Kenya, on a Government-sponsored colonizing scheme, which settled ex-soldiers on pieces of virgin land for the payment of a few pounds.

I can only assume that his reason for calling the farm 'Porgies' was an ironic Edwardian joke. The Small Porgies, a character in one of Kipling's *Just So Stories*, is an enormous creature who periodically rises out of the sea and consumes all the produce of the land. The farm did in the end consume everything that Father possessed, but, hopeless farmer though he was, he could not have known this in 1922.

To his children, of course, it was a perfect place to grow. We had the run of the place; it was on Porgies that I first became conscious of things; and it was of Porgies that I thought with an ache, as I walked into that high dark hall at Allesley, where there were lots of people smiling down at me, the women in long dresses and the men all looking like stewards. Ailie, unerringly instinctive, whisked me upstairs with Duff to the schoolroom (I was told it was), where I was given bread and milk and cocoa in front of the huge brass fireguard, with towels warming over one end of it. So this was home. Duff smiled and fussed and clucked round me. But this – was home. It was rather chilly for home.

II

THE 'RELIGIOUS, ROYAL AND ANCIENT FOUNDATION' OF Christ's Hospital came into being by an edict of the boy king Edward VI in 1552. The object of the exercise was to provide grammar school education for the clever sons of hard-up clergy, half-pay naval officers and worthy but penurious members of the struggling classes. In fact, a rather up-market charity school. Its original location was in Newgate Street in the City of London, but that plot was sold to the Post Office, and in 1902 a new school was built outside Horsham in Sussex. However, Christ's Hospital has never broken its links with the City, and a large number of boys – and girls now – have links with London parishes and boroughs; and on St Matthew's Day every year, the senior school led by the school band, in full regalia, marches through the City to the Mansion House.

In the four and a half centuries since its foundation many distinguished alumni have owed their education to Christ's Hospital. Samuel Coleridge, Charles Lamb, Leigh Hunt, Edmund Blunden, Barnes Wallis, Sir Colin Davis, Bernard

Levin – the list is long, and catholic. But perhaps 'Housey's' most solid achievement has been to feed into the professions a steady stream of well-qualified, honourable, but unsung practitioners who, but for the school, might never have had the opportunity to develop their talents. 'And some there be who have no memorial; who are perished as though they had never been . . . But their name liveth for evermore.'

This passage from Ecclesiasticus was read, appropriately, by the Senior Grecian in chapel every Speech Day. Few gatherings of professional men – businessmen, dons or churchmen, doctors, lawyers, engineers or whatever – would not find among their number a fair sprinkling of Old Blues. (Blue is the colour of the long coat worn over the knee-breeches and yellow stockings of the romantic Elizabethan uniform still proudly worn today – though I did once hear a woman in Coventry who saw me in my uniform say to her companion: 'That's a reformatory boy.')

Eton, Harrow, Winchester and the other great English schools have provided the backbone and the leadership of the English class system. Christ's Hospital's distinction has been to leaven the lump with a constant flow of high-calibre recruits from every sort of background and its tentacles now spread around the globe.

One of these tentacles reached round Africa to the Crown Colony of Kenya; and every seven years – the time span of a Housey education – this tentacle picked out one boy from the colony's European schools, and offered him a scholarship. In 1936 this treasure was awarded to me, for reasons which have always been a mystery; I do not recall having to work for it at all.

The outcome was that in the fall of that year – the year of the Spanish Civil War, Mussolini's invasion of Abyssinia, and the abdication of Edward VIII – I sailed from Kenya, alone, aged ten, and did not return or see my parents again for twenty years. I suppose I am only now seeing the many ways in which I was affected by the culture shock, not that it matters much now; but for my mother, my leaving home was appalling. She told me that it was like an amputation. I rather think that Father took it in his stride, as he did everything else.

At all events, mixed though the blessings may have been, I am keenly aware of the advantages to me of what happened. I received, entirely free, from Christ's Hospital, an education that could not have been found in Africa north of the Cape, even if Father could have afforded it, which, considering the sort of schooling my siblings received, is extremely doubtful. My debt to the school is profound, and my later years there were happy ones. But at first it was a bit too big. Plunging into the routine of a huge impersonal institution was like entering a dark tunnel, full of confusing noise, much too fast. Suddenly life became serious; a high standard of work was expected; the nose was introduced to the grindstone; and games were played on enormous fields full of competitors. Actions began to have consequences. I was about to learn that chilblains can itch as much as jiggers, and you can feel just as sick in Taunton as in Timbuctoo.

The point is that long before I knew any of this, England

was to me a kind of fairyland. 'Home' we called it, and anything that smacked of home was imbued with magic. The taste of an apple that has been cut in half can still take me back to childhood; for apples were a luxury, grown only with difficulty in the cooler districts, and given as special presents. We never had enough to go round. The garden at Porgies was loaded with every kind of exotic fruit – guavas, passion fruit, mangoes, bananas, pawpaws, custard apples and loquats. But an apple meant England and England, I was convinced, was like a great green cushion: if you fell over in England you could not possibly graze your knees.

This was an important fact of life. Gravel rash was an unpleasant and permanent hazard. Not to have it, and smell of Zambuk all the time, was a consummation devoutly to be wished. It outweighed almost anything. Elgon's majestic snow-capped peaks or the flamingo-fringed jewel that was Lake Nakuru were mere bits of old wasteland when set against my sisters' remembered accounts of the Jephson Gardens in Leamington. Those soft lawns and moist, buxom flower beds full of salvia and marigolds sounded like a corner of paradise. Some years later, with Elastoplast on both knees from a fall off my bicycle, I sought out and took a walk in those same Jephson Gardens. It is not really a criticism to say that it was then that nostalgia for Africa set hard in my heart.

On a gently rising piece of ground, facing the blue hills of the Trans-Nzoia, Father built a long, low, shambling bungalow. It had walls of mud and wattle, and a corrugated iron roof on which the pied wagtails skittered about all day whistling, their little sharp claws sounding like light rain. There had been an earlier house, of thatch, before I was born, but it had caught a flying spark one morning and gone up in smoke. All that remained of it was a line of charred posts forming a creeper-covered trellis in what was now a sort of back garden.

The rooms were large and airy, with beaten earth and cowdung floors in the African manner – floorboards would have stood no chance against the white ants – and were kept shady by the wide shallow verandah which wrapped round two sides of the house. The front door led straight into the living room, and the mat outside it was as far as the dogs (and the *totos*) were allowed. At one end of this room was a large dining table in a window recess, which looked right down the garden. The walls were hung with hunting trophies, a painting of Stellenbosch (mine, this: a present from my godmother who was called Mrs Molesworth, which is all I know about her; I don't ever remember meeting her) and some lovely Persian rugs – loot from my father's army service in Mesopotamia. My mother's treadle Singer sewing machine was against one wall; and there were comfortable rawhide armchairs and a huge bulbous sofa which usually had my eldest sister, Marion, draped over it, palely reading Warwick Deeping or Dornford Yates and crying at the sentimental bits.

The kitchen, my mother's power base, was dark and smoky, its roof beams stained dark brown from the old wood-fired range. I loved it – there was always something going on and endless chatter from the Africans crowding round the back door, and shouting banter to whoever was working there. I used to know when Mummy was baking bread, because the legs of the locally cobbled table creaked loudly from her kneading. I would be in there like a flash, to poke my finger into the top of the dough in the baking tins – her loaves always had a sort of navel in the top – or to lick clean the cake mixture left in the bowl.

My mother did all her own cooking. This was unusual among white people, even ones as poor as we were, for labour was cheap and African cooks were often adept and full of imagination. Her decision to do so sprang from the evening when, finding the gravy missing from the dinner table, she went into the kitchen just in time to see the cook mopping it up from the floor with a dishcloth and squeezing it back into the gravy boat. She was wont to say that it was not prejudice, just a question of knowing where the food had been.

At the other end of the house were the bedrooms – four of them. The big one was the parents' room, with a huge double bed and – my mother's pride and joy – a large Victorian tall-boy which had come from part of her distant family. Behind this room was another smaller room which Dorothy, Patricia and I shared. And, squeezed down the end of the house, were two tiny rooms for Dick and Marion, the eldest. Over each bed hung from the ceiling a contraption that looked like a large turban during the day. This was the mosquito net, let down at night and tucked in all the way round, so that you slept in a sort of cage. This essential piece of equipment was not simply to protect us from the anopheles mosquito, which carried the malarial infection, but to guard against all the other biting, stinging or just fluttery things which could make the night unwholesome.

In a sort of L behind the house and down one side, my mother, a passionate gardener, had planted some eucalyptus trees back in 1922 when the family had first come to the farm.

By the time I was taking notice of things, these trees already formed an efficient windbreak. Tall and gaunt, with pale grey bark forever peeling off in strips like sunburnt skin, they had narrow, wonderful smelling leaves and silly fluffy flowers like tiny pink chicks. The lemon gums were the home of countless weaver-birds, whose hanging nests festooned the branches like drab Christmas decorations. Weaver-birds are about the size of starlings, gold and black, with pale, inquisitive eyes. Gregarious and domesticated, they are eternally attending to their nests, chattering and whistling from morning till night. 'Like ladies at a parish party,' Father said. Their squabbling, and the skittering and piping of the wagtails on the tin roof, were the daytime background noises of Porgies. These, and the monotonous 'green gravel, green gravel' cooing of the ring-doves. Of course, the short sharp rainstorms in the wet season overcame all other sounds with their deafening drum-beats, but these only lasted a brief while, and the birds took over again.

Among the lemon gums my mother had planted a couple of flamboyant trees, which grew high and elegant and produced handsome blood-red, trumpet-shaped flowers. I spent many hours high in the branches of the flamboyants, watching the tiny, shot-silk humming birds hovering at the blossoms, burying their long curved beaks deep inside in search of nectar. Sometimes I killed one with my catapult, and gave it to Dick to add to his collection of stuffed birds. I don't think Dick appreciated my gifts very much: they were so tiny. Even his neat fingers found them too fiddly.

I remember the front of the house as having a certain dignity, not to say grandeur; a wide gravel driveway swept round a sumptuous flower bed full of zinnias and canna lilies; but a faded snapshot gives the lie to my fantasy. The gravel drive is of caked earth, sprouting everywhere with grass and weeds. The flower bed is there all right, but the flowers look as if they could do with a drink. And the house, its roof sagging a bit here and there, looks as if it is having a hard struggle against the encroachments of the bush.

On the other side of the driveway was a large border, overgrown with shrubs and creepers, and beyond that sloped a piece of what I suppose had once been intended as a lawn, but lack of attention had reduced it to an overgrown paddock, full of butterflies, and choked with a weed we called blackjack. This plant grew burrs like black caraway seeds, as persistent as a pub bore – they simply would not be brushed off. Each one had to be picked off clothes, hair and eyebrows and carefully disposed of, or it would fly back like an iron filing to a magnet.

Beyond this scrubby patch was a spreading mango and a tall guava tree, and then the garden proper, a wonderful wilderness full of secret spots and corners.

It bore no relation to the majestic English-type gardens which I had seen in the White Highlands, so familiar from pictures of the life of British settlers in Kenya. Not for us the stately cedars spreading gravely over well-shaved lawns, or bougainvillea and frangipani tastefully placed beside weedless paths. We had bougainvillea and frangipani, to be sure, but they took their chance in the higgledy-piggledy acre or so of fruit trees, vines, shrubs, flowers and vegetables off which we lived and in which we played endlessly. Certainly it was worked in and loved by my mother and, for some time, by Kunani, the garden 'boy'; otherwise, the bush would soon have claimed it back; but they had little time for anything but the most basic fundamentals of husbandry. A cornucopia of tropical fruit and vegetables jostled for light and air against a host of shrubs and vines and flowers, which tumbled and climbed all over the place. It was ravishing, but dangerous too, for it was a haven for snakes, so we always had to be wary. It must have been a permanent anxiety for my mother; she was forever telling us to 'watch out for snakes'; as I never wore shoes, I must have seemed very vulnerable. I never went out without her warning, 'Don't walk in the long grass,' being called after me.

Occasionally we were a bit careless. One evening a puff adder hissed a warning at me as I was about to pick it up, mistaking it for a piece of firewood, and sometimes a snake would be found curled up in the cool bathroom on a hot afternoon. Once my sister Tricia came face to face with a large green mamba in the branches of the guava tree, which she had climbed in search of fruit. Instinct saved her life and she only sprained her ankle, for she simply let go of her branch and fell out of the tree to the ground.

Father was away at the time and Mother, who feared snakes just a little more than she feared firearms, went for the shotgun.

The cornering or treeing of a dangerous snake was a sufficiently rare occurrence to attract a crowd, and there is nothing an African loves more than a drama. The tree was soon surrounded, not just by us children, but by every African on the *shamba*. Besides, the killing of such a venomous creature as a mamba would be the excuse for a celebration. I do not remember anyone in Africa – black or white – ignoring a deadly snake and letting it go on its way. I suppose the danger of it bruising their heels was too close for them to forego the pleasure of bruising its head.

Mother came out of the house, preceded at arm's length by Father's big twelve bore. She spotted the green snake staring balefully down at the circle of people. Its head swayed gently. She managed to pull back the hammers and cock the gun and raised it uncertainly to her shoulder. Just as she was about to pull the trigger one of the African houseboys leapt in front of her and pointed an excited finger at the tree.

'There it is, memsah'b,' he shouted. Mother was already pulling the trigger and only had time to point the barrels at the sky. The gun went off with a roar, the African fainted, and Mother sat down heavily from the recoil. The snake was never seen again. I do not recall any of us climbing that guava tree again either. The snake's camouflage was too effective for that particular shade of green.

Usually, of course, snakes get out of the way before they are seen. They are no more enamoured of the human race than we are of them – and with far more cause. If people would only remember that snakes only attack when they feel threatened, maybe we would be less paranoid towards them, and we could all rub along a great deal better. Mother knew this all too well. She came from Australia, where snakes were far more in evidence, and her daily, 'Don't walk in the long grass,' made us automatically wary. At all events, the garden was a most attractive playground, and none of us felt in undue danger. Innocence is, of course, a great protector. There was a later occasion when, now the proud possessor of a .22 rifle, I was intrigued to hear a lot of birds making an unusual amount of noise inside a small thicket. I tiptoed up to the thicket, looking for a good shot. (I blazed away at anything in those days.) I actually had my rifle to my shoulder and was stepping back to get a better sighting when my sister Marion screamed. I was so startled that I pulled the trigger and a huge black snake whistled between my legs into the thicket. Marion had come out of the house, to see me quietly backing onto the snake, which was reared back, ready to strike. Her scream and the shot had been enough to make it change its mind and escape. And I learnt a lesson: if birds are calling in alarm, be wary – something is alarming them.

The fruit in the garden proved a boon in our fairly frequent times of poverty, for there was always something to eat throughout the year. We used to get up in the morning and, still in our pyjamas, dash about the garden with large soup plates, which we filled with our own selection of fruit for breakfast. Custard apples were my favourite, green scaly-looking things about the size of a pear, with white creamy flesh and shiny black seeds. It did actually taste quite like custard.

Beyond the fruit trees was the vegetable patch: a rather arid area, open and stony, I seem to remember, and shaded by a few pawpaw trees. These were tall, palm-like trees with a sprouting of spatulate leaves at the top. The pawpaws grew in clusters at the base of these leaves, like coconuts, greeny-yellow and the size of a melon.

Actually, I don't suppose the pawpaws were as tall as all that; in fact, I think I can remember Dick reaching them from the ground. But they seemed miles away to me.

This part of the garden was the particular province of Kunani, the garden boy. 'Boy' is a misnomer, for Kunani was gnarled and elderly, but the word 'boy' was used in those days as a generic term for any African. When, a few years later, I came to England and was told to 'go and play with the boys', I was a little startled; the people I played with were 'totos' in my language. 'Boys' were grown up.

Kunani was tall and blue-black, with aquiline features and piercing eyes, quite unlike the flat-nosed, cheery-faced members of the local Kitosh. I suspect he had Arab blood somewhere in his veins – he was probably of Somali extraction – but no-one seemed to know anything about him. He was thought to be something of a witch doctor, for he always had peculiar things hanging from his belt that could well have been charms. At all events, he kept himself to himself, and there was certainly something mysterious about him. The local Africans distrusted and feared him.

But I loved him. I could always make him laugh. He would listen to my prattle for a while, solemnly, like an old vulture, then he would slap his gaunt shanks, shoot an accurate gobbet of spittle at some passing insect, and go off into a rather sinister high-pitched chuckle, which sometimes went on for minutes. I spent a lot of time playing near him, and he would explain about plants and roots and animals, as he scratched about in the garden, or squatted under a tree, smoking his horrible smelly old pipe. This pipe had a personality all its own. Kunani had made it himself out of a length of aluminium tubing screwed into the hollowed-out lump of some local equivalent of briar. It was filthy and stained and dottle-ridden. What he smoked in it, I never asked. He would produce an unspeakable old pouch from some secret part of his anatomy and pour a sort of greenish-brown dust into the bowl, tamp it down with a claw-like finger, light up, and settle into a trance-like reverie, keening gently to himself.

My first steps as a smoker had to do, indirectly, with Kunani's pipe. I cannot have been more than five when I stole some of Father's 'King Stork' cigarettes, to smoke with my friends behind the bean rows. I do not recall once being sick as a result of smoking, but I knew perfectly well that it was a forbidden pleasure. Because of this, I chewed sprigs of mint to disguise my breath when I was called into lunch. But children seldom succeed in deceiving grown-ups. They invariably slip up on some elementary piece of tactics. I must have been seen furtively picking the mint and cramming it into my mouth. Whatever it was, when I arrived at the house I was confronted by the entire family and asked why I was eating all that mint. I liked mint, I said innocently. I suppose I must have reeked of tobacco, for my mother's next question took my breath away.

'Have you been smoking?'

I can remember very clearly thinking out my excuse; danger concentrates the mind wonderfully. I had a brilliant flash of inspiration. I had had a puff or two of Kunani's pipe, I said. Genius.

Not so. My mother knew perfectly well that I was lying. She gave an excellent imitation of shock and horror. I had doubtless been poisoned, she said, and must have no lunch, for that would simply push the poison deep down into my system. Instead, I must bring it up straight away.

I was stuck with my lie, and had no alternative but to comply. So we all acted out a ludicrous charade, which I have no doubt everyone enjoyed but me. They all went through the motions of deep concern for my health, while I had to drink a whole glass of warm salt water – which, of course, promptly made me sick. I was then put to bed – which made me cross – and I have since been told that it caused the family great amusement.

I like to think that it was an instinct for dramatic

consistency that made me play out the whole silly drama, and not admit to my sin. Many is the bad play I have been in, which it was sinful to do in the first place, but which could only be done by playing it out to the final curtain as if one believed in it.

One lesson I did learn, though, and not a very creditable one: it taught me to be much more careful next time I wanted a smoke.

My friendship with Kunani had a sad end, and one of which I am not very proud. As I grew older – that is, when I stopped being a baby and began to be a little boy – I began to make friends with the African children on the farm. Wanyonyi was my special friend at that time, and I became part of a group for the first time in my life. To my embarrassment, I discovered that Kunani had an unsavoury reputation among the *totos*, who had all been ordered by their parents to have nothing to do with him. Dark suggestions were put into my mind of witchcraft and the casting of spells – there were even hints of a murder or two in the past. Who was he? Where had he come from? Was I sure it was the serval cats that stole the chickens?

Even my parents did not know the answers when finally I asked them. He had turned up on the farm one day and asked for work. His *kipandi* – a sort of identity-cum-reference card – seemed to be in order, and my mother needed someone to help in the garden. He was taken on and it soon became clear that he had a way with growing things.

He built himself a hut in an isolated spot near the bottom of the garden and there he lived, all alone, apparently minding his own business; certainly not encouraging anyone else to mind it for him.

Apart from the fact of his being 'different' and a 'foreigner', it was this self-imposed isolation, I suspect, that was the basis for his unsavoury reputation among the local Africans, because nothing could ever be positively pinned on him, and his work was always good and reliable. But he had no friends, he took no wives – and he certainly had an individual look about him. In fact, he was a very striking, rather aristocratic figure, as he went about the garden, stooped and predatory-looking, drawing on his filthy old pipe.

The pressure of the group was far too strong for me and so gradually my new friends weaned me of my old one, and my affection for Kunani turned to suspicion, dislike, and finally to fear.

I wish I could remember what it was that brought about the final crisis. I am told that he put a curse on me. It was probably my fault; I am quite likely to have hurled a stone at him, or something. Whatever it was, Kunani became more isolated and cranky. He had never been particularly amenable, and had been known to argue heatedly with my mother, locking himself up in his hut for two or three days at a time, in a great sulk. But now he became quite alarming and took to abusing us whenever we went into the garden. It got to be quite scary.

Finally, it was clear that he would have to go, and Father dismissed him. He was forbidden the farm and told never to come back. We heard dark rumours of his lurking about, making sinister signs at the house and burning little effigies, but we never actually saw him again. We burnt down his hut in, as I recall, an almost exorcistic ritual, one evening after sunset. And danced round the flames.

As I write this, I am astonished at it, but it is such a vivid memory that I am sure it happened. We must have become very frightened of him. It was certainly a great relief to me when he disappeared. But my mother always said he was the best gardener she had ever had.

At the very bottom of the garden, about three hundred yards from the house, was a small banana plantation, which Father had established when the place was young. Banana trees are odd – not trees at all really. The trunk is made up of the compacted stems of the huge smooth leaves which fan out at the top like a palm tree. The great bunches of fruit grow out of the middle of all this and hang there in a way that always seemed to me to be upside down, with the fruit pointing upwards instead of to the ground.

Banana leaves have all sorts of uses for the African – from roofing material to food containers to termite traps. When what we called the white ants took to the wing at the start of the rains, the Kitosh used to build smooth banana-leaf chutes at the exit holes on top of the anthills. Then they would sit on top of the hill, at an improvised drum made out of a hollowed log, and beat a persistent and repetitive gentle rhythm on it with two sticks. This made the ants think that the rains had arrived. They would then queue up in their thousands, ready to fly, and slide down the slippery banana leaf helter-skelter into waiting bowls, to be consumed alive in handfuls, or taken away to be dried. Flying termites were regarded as a great delicacy – still are, for all I know. I could never quite bring myself to eat one alive, but I often nibbled them after they had been dried in the sun; and very delicious they are, like little nuts.

There was always great excitement when the white ants flew. The air was full of electricity as the rains approached, with great dark clouds building up in the mountains, and the insistent beating of the drums filling everywhere with rhythm. Everyone seemed restless and my heart always beat with expectation. Birds – black swifts, brown kites, rainbow-coloured bee-eaters and a host of others – flew screaming round the anthills, picking off the ants that escaped the traps. Yet, still enough got away to form new colonies.

The *totos* had fun too, hurling short, knobbed sticks at the birds as they circled the anthills. Some of them developed remarkable skill at this and several sad bundles of feathers tumbled to earth, to be eaten later, skewered and toasted over the fire at the back of the house. The boy who drove the ox-team had a long rawhide whip, which was cracked over the heads of the oxen to encourage them to greater efforts. I remember his cracking this, too, at the circling birds, quite often flicking one out of the sky.

It was all very barbaric and exciting and I suppose it was Nature balancing her books, as it were. If there had not been this annual termite massacre, Africa would quickly have been reduced to a dust bowl, consumed from one end to the other by the ubiquitous white ant.

It was a strange place, the banana plantation – silent and green and secret. The few birds there were different from the ones elsewhere on the farm – the bright, raucous, swanky creatures that flew arrogantly about outside. These were grey ghosts that slipped quietly between the trunks and disappeared slyly into the undergrowth. There was one bird we called the swamp-pheasant – a brown, long-tailed creature which hid itself in the dark green gloom and only sang when there was rain about, a cello-like song, full of foreboding. It was not well named, for, though it looked rather like a pheasant, it was smelly and quite inedible. I suppose it had its own natural predators; everything does in the balance of nature. But whatever it was, it must have had peculiar tastes.

I never liked to go into the bananas alone. There was an eerie feeling about the place. I always felt that I was being watched. Perhaps I was, and perhaps it was my wise mother doing the watching. She kept us all alive on the sale of these bananas when the farm was on its last legs, and Father was digging holes all over the place in the optimistic, but unavailing, search for gold. On the subject of watching: there was a small knoll at the far edge of the banana plantation. From the top of it there was a good view of the maize fields beyond. Here Father built himself a simple shelter where he could sit in the shade and oversee the boys working in the maize. He would sit there, balanced on a shooting stick, talking and laughing, when suddenly he would leap to his feet and go charging off into the fields, limping furiously, to take it out on some poor unfortunate African who had taken an unscheduled break to have a pee. For a kindly, gentle man, he was sometimes very bad-tempered.

This little knoll had a very satisfactory slide down one side and in the wet weather we used to toboggan down its muddy slopes, sitting astride a fine slippery banana trunk.

It was also one of the favourite exercise places for Bumpity Kate.

At the back of the house, and fed by the roof gutters, were two enormous, corrugated-iron rainwater tanks, each holding, I suppose, about five hundred gallons. They were the household's main source of fresh water. Bumpity Kate had once been such a tank, attached to the old house when it burned down. As a result, she was ruptured and punctured beyond repair and, for a time, she became my siblings' favourite plaything. They turned her on her side, climbed in, and walked up the inside walls, making the old tank trundle along like a huge cotton reel. Dick and the three girls had endless, clattering fun in Bumpity Kate. I was scared of her, though; I was too small, and found it hard to keep my balance when the thing really got moving. For it was fraught with danger. When Bumpity Kate had been punctured, there were jagged bits of metal sticking up inside her. It was no fun at all to fall and slide into one of these excrescences as she rolled about the farm. So I rather missed out on the heyday of Bumpity Kate. By the time I was ready to cope with the problems of balance, the others had grown out of her. I was too small to cope with her on my own, and

36

my African friends regarded her with deep suspicion for some reason. So Bumpity Kate rusted gently away, overgrown with creepers and nested in by birds and snakes and creepy-crawlies.

There was another tank at the back of the house. This was smaller than the others, and stood on four stout brick pillars against the house wall. A pipe from this tank led straight through the wall to the long tin bath which stood against the wall on the other side.

Under this tank was a great wood fire which never went out. The purpose of this was to heat the water for the bwanas' baths, but it was also, and importantly, the gathering place for all the Africans on the *boma* and was one of my favourite spots. A *boma* was originally a thick thorn hedge to protect the homestead from the incursions of wild animals, and came to represent the homestead itself. Here in the dark there was always a ring of black faces glistening in the firelight, and there was laughter and chatter and animated discussion. Here they roasted sweet potatoes in the hot ashes, or toasted bits of meat on wooden skewers; and here they sang their repetitive, rhythmical songs:

> *Moja, mbili, tatu,*
> *Nyangau na kula viatu.*
> *Viatu na lia,*
> *Nyangau na kimbia,*
> *Moja, mbili, tatu.*

One, two, three,
Hyenas gnaw the shoes,
The shoes give cry,
Hyenas fly.
One, two, three.

The hyena, known for its cowardly opportunism, will eat anything it comes upon. This was a popular song, and always raised a laugh.

They needed a fire, for at that altitude – about three thousand feet above sea level – the nights became very chilly. When the sun went down, light and warmth were quickly gone and the men would squat close to the fire, the old ones wrapped in their inevitable soft blankets, while the children tumbled about and the women went busily back and forth from the huts, doing all the domestic chores.

Whenever Father or Dick shot a buck or bought a sheep for slaughter, the animal was strung up to the lowest branch of one of the flamboyant trees, for skinning and butchering. When the joints and the head, the heart, kidneys and liver had been removed to the house, the rest of the carcass was left for the boys, who hacked chunks off and grilled them straight-away over the fire. Very fresh meat, barbecued on the spot like this is extremely tough, but the flavour is wonderful. If it was a sheep that had been killed, I begged for, and was often given, the fat tail to grill, for it guttered and spat most satisfactorily and tasted divine. These were moments of total contentment, squatting there among my friends, my eyeballs getting uncomfortable from the heat, listening to the endless chatter. The dogs, Porge and Smudge, lay on the outskirts of the ring, their eyes catching the firelight, waiting to have the tough gristly bits thrown to them. A quick gobble and swallow, no time wasted, and back again, poised, ready for the next gobbet.

Sometimes, on fine nights when the huge tropical moon sailed straight overhead, so close you felt you could touch it, I took a cushion and went apart to a place by myself and lay on the ground and gazed up at it. I have no idea what made me do it, except that I was always wondering what lay beyond infinity. It always made me cry, not unhappily, but with a delicious melancholy.

III

ALLESLEY RECTORY WAS A BIG UGLY HOUSE WITH LONG dark corridors and, apart from open fires in some of the rooms, the entire source of heat came from a large and ancient cosy stove in the cavernous hall, which burned anthracite and smelled of farts when the wind was in the prevailing quarter. On my first morning I caused some mirth by coming down to breakfast (very sensibly, I thought) in my fine new woollen gloves. I had only just learnt that cold could hurt.

Washing, too, was a strain. Bobby showed me the boys' bathroom. Halfway down a dark corridor, you turned left. In front of you was the loo, a majestic room with a shiny mahogany bench with a hole in the middle, and a copy of Rupert Brooke's collected works beside the *Izal* toilet roll. The pan was of blue patterned china, which always intrigued me; was one supposed to turn round afterwards and admire it? I did, and the water swirling about looked very clean and blue. Perhaps that was the point.

If you turned left again before the loo, there were two shiny oak steps down to a large cold room with a slippery oak floor; a room full of cupboards and tables and ironing boards, with a large deep sink under the window, and a huge uncompromising bath down one wall.

The water in the mornings was never very hot, and on that first day, Bobby was determined to show how hardy he was by splashing about noisily, stripped to the waist.

I had a poor shot at copying him, but my hands were numb and clumsy with cold, and I only succeeded in making my pyjama trousers very wet. This amused him for some reason, and he chased me back down the corridor to get my circulation going again. I had already fallen under his spell, for he was warm and friendly under the banter, and had not held my remark about the steward against me. This was just as well, because I was destined to share his room, and, being four years older and that much bigger than me, he could have made life difficult. But, apart from occasionally swinging me round his head to teach me manners, or sitting me down and making me repeat, 'How now, thou brown cow', to rid me of my East African twang, he put up with my invasion and I grew to love him.

His father, Rupert Winser – the Rector, as I came to call him, because I could not bring myself to call him 'Uncle' – was a gentle, kind and unworldly man whose shyness made him an embarrassment to me. He was supposed to have suffered from shell-shock as a chaplain in the trenches, which may have accounted for his eccentricities. He was given to telling frightful unfunny jokes and laughing uproariously at them. I would laugh politely, but the rest of the family just said, 'Oh, Daddy . . .', which made him blush and look crestfallen.

At table, two things about him always fascinated me. The first was his habit, when pouring out a glass of water, only ever to half-fill the glass. Perhaps he was conditioned by some long-past drought that no-one else remembered. The other was his method with toast and marmalade. Instead of spreading his toast, as I had learnt to do, he would break off a tiny piece and load it with an enormous lump of butter and an equally enormous dollop of marmalade, pop the whole lot in his mouth and munch away. He got a bit of stick for it from Ailie during the years of rationing, but it has always seemed to me a most satisfactory example to follow.

The rest of the family were not due home till Christmas. Philip, the eldest, was away at college somewhere; Freddy, the second son, was in his last year at Rugby and rang up on the morning after I arrived to find out what I sounded like. I could not think why he insisted on speaking to me – we had nothing to say to each other. The youngest, Susan, was at a girls' prep school in Leamington called New College. So I was spared the effort of getting to know the whole family at one gulp.

Without doubt, however, the dynamo of the household was my father's horse-faced cousin, Ailie, full of laughter, charm and firm opinions. I soon learnt that 'I am not arguing with you – I – KNOW,' was a clear signal to button my opinionated lip, however sure I was of my facts. Someone once said of her that she had a first-rate relationship with God, just so long as God did what she told Him. She preferred male company – 'I can always make men laugh.' Women either worshipped her, or avoided her. She sang a lot (mostly tra-la-la-ing Edwardian music hall songs), had no patience with ditherers, and always made snap decisions. I had never come across anyone like her before and, though I have never been able to decide how much I liked her, there is no doubt she inspired my worship, and I trusted her utterly. It was my good fortune to have landed, almost by accident, amongst this good, kindly family, swirled along by such a forceful, high-principled and funny lady. I find it hard to imagine what my life would have been like if I had had to live with Duff in her dark, steep little house in Leamington, with epileptic Norah and the 'getting on' Mrs Townsend. That was where my happy-go-lucky, charming father still thought I was living. He probably gave a characteristic chuckle when he heard that I was settled with his rather racy cousin Ailie, with whom he had danced the Lancers at civic balls in Coventry before the war. But Coventry was a long way from Kenya, and Kenya life was full of improvisations.

My brother, Richard, was twelve years older than I and, even as a child, he had never been a lightweight. His second fairy-cycle had had to be custom-made, because he had bent the frame of his first.

He was lazy, amiable and slow to anger, with a big boy's fondness for little things; he had an extraordinary neatness with his fingers. When he was about fifteen he made a model farm for our sister, Dorothy, who had been ill. It was a miracle of tiny paper ducks and chickens; it was an English farm, of course. England was always 'home'. There were delicate wooden fences and cows and sheep made of painted cork. Dorothy kept it for many years, because I can clearly remember the duckpond of silver paper with a realistic fringe of reeds made out of the chopped and dyed bristles from an old scrubbing brush. I can still see his great moon face as he bent over some intricate piece of work, blowing noisily through his big shiny nose and whistling tunelessly in concentration. I envied him his talent, for I was never handy enough to acquire that sort of skill. I usually end up with more glue on my fingers and eyebrows than ever gets onto the cup I am supposed to be mending.

Dick's great passion was lepidopterology, the study of butterflies and moths. In time he became an amateur authority on East African butterflies and his collection was one of the largest in Kenya. I can never get a whiff of camphor without seeing his little room at Porgies, its wide window sill laden with breeding cages, killing bottles and all the paraphernalia of the butterfly collector. If only he could have managed to acquire a few qualifications, he could have become professionally the bug expert that undoubtedly he was. But he lacked the drive and ambition to take him there, and Father lacked the money – and the drive, too – to get them for him. So his hopes were always foundering in a mess of lost opportunities. Of course, this applied to his love life as well; a more hopeful, but hopeless, courtier there can hardly ever have been. Because of this – and naturally his size did not help him to be taken seriously – he was referred to always as 'poor old Dick'. He seemed jovial enough, though I suspect he had long ago learnt the fat person's defence tactic of playing the clown. Laugh and the world laughs with you . . .

Nevertheless, I am grateful to my brother. He kindled in me an interest in butterflies and birds which has given me pleasure all through my life. I can still recognize and remember many African butterflies by their sonorous Latin names. I used to be quite pompous about it. In my first summer in England I refused to take our native British butterflies seriously. Not only did I find them drab and boring, but their names were too childish. How could one give a Peacock or a Meadow Brown the same scientific respect as *Papilio Dardanus* or *Charaxes Pollux Pollux*? *Dardanus* was a large, glamorous, floppy beauty, yellow and black with long tails, and it seemed to lower his aristocratic credentials when I learnt that he is related to our own native Swallowtail. What a name to give a butterfly! As for *Pollux*, he belongs to the wonderful buccaneering *Charaxes* family. Nothing like him in England. The genus *Charaxes* are the eagles of the butterfly world. They circle the tops of their favourite trees and fight each other to rags with their strong saw-fronted forewings. Difficult to catch, too, I remember, because of their speed and wide-awakeness and the fact that they seldom come down low enough to be within reach of the net.

Dick would watch a female butterfly for hours, noting the places where she settled and then send Omari, his special 'butterfly boy', shinning up into the branches to collect the leaves, in the hope that she had laid an egg on one of them.

My personal favourite of all the butterflies I saw, Dick called *Cymathoë Hobarti*. (This meant that a Mr Hobart had discovered that particular scion of the *Cymathoë* family. Who was Mr Hobart, I wonder? Dick would have known.) *Hobarti* is a brilliant little beauty from the forests, bright scarlet on its upper side and brown-leaf camouflage underneath. I caught one once and bore it, still fluttering inside my net, excitedly to my brother. Dick took it out gently, examined it cursorily and let it go, to my intense fury. He explained patiently that it was a badly damaged specimen and he had a much better spare in his collection that he could let me have. He did not seem to understand that that was not the same thing and pooh-poohed my frustration. I could cheerfully have sliced his head off.

When he found some eggs that he wanted, Dick would watch over them till they hatched and place them in a breeding cage with fresh supplies of the correct food plant for the tiny caterpillars. Then he would carefully rescue the minute egg-case and stick it neatly on a piece of card. He did the same with the caterpillar skin each time it was shed as the thing grew and finally, when the butterfly emerged, the chrysalis case followed suit. He now had a complete record of all the stages in its development, which he placed in his specimen cabinets, beside the perfect example of the butterfly itself, killed and set before it could do itself any harm.

I made sporadic efforts to emulate Dick's methods with my

hopeless collection, but I never succeeded in breeding any-thing from egg to imago. There were so many hazards: if you did not put fresh food plants in the cage every day, they would wither and the caterpillars would starve; if you forgot to place a piece of cardboard over the water jar with a hole only just big enough for the stem to pass through, sure as hell the caterpillars – my caterpillars, anyway – would fall in and drown. If you left the cage open for more than the shortest time, an ichneumon fly might get in and lay an egg on the wretched caterpillar. If that happened, then when the egg hatched the ensuing grub ate its way into the host and my carefully nurtured caterpillar, instead of turning into a chrysalis, would burst and out would come a mean-looking wasp-like animal, truly a wolf in sheep's clothing.

I sometimes wondered how the wretched things survived under their own steam in the wild, so vulnerable were they. Dick would patiently explain about the balance of nature and the survival of the fittest, but it seemed long odds to me. More often, of course, I would simply kill the poor little things out of carelessness, by squishing them with a clumsy thumb, or putting something on top of them. Many a tear I shed over my battered collection.

Dick's collection, however, became well-known among the cognoscenti in Nairobi, especially so when he actually bred a variant female of a fairly common butterfly, the males and females of which were thought to be identical. This creature was officially renamed *Charaxes Ethiocles Evansi*, and Dick achieved a tiny corner of immortality. Perhaps some latter-day lepidopterist will ask: 'Who was Evans, I wonder?' He was a great big amiable twenty-stoner in khaki slacks and bush-jacket, with little ambition and endless patience, who had the deftest fingers I ever knew.

Under Dick's scornful but tolerant guidance, I would trot about the farm, armed with a little butterfly net made by my mother out of mosquito netting, sweeping into it anything that came within reach and carefully popping my catches into the small paper envelopes which Dick had made for me. Usually my specimens were worthless to him; either he had them already, or they were so battered as to be unrecognizable. On the rare occasions when I did catch something he wanted, it caused a certain tension. I would swell with pride at having caught something he had not seen before, but, at the same time, I would want to keep it, just because he hadn't got it. This was where Father would step in and point out the likelihood of my making a mess of it. Dick invariably won it in the end.

For, a proper mess I made of my butterflies, and my collecting case was spattered with tears of frustration. I would faithfully go through the laborious process of setting out, trying to do as Dick did. It was a delicate exercise. The dried corpse, its wings closed from lying in its little envelope for several days, had to be floated in a cup of hot water, with a pin stuck into its thorax to act as a centre-board, so that it sailed on the surface like a tiny yacht. When the steam had softened it, it was pinned out on a setting-board, its wings spread prettily, held down with little strips of paper. It was then left to dry out again.

This was the bit I never mastered. When Dick did it, it took him about fifteen seconds; he would make no mark on the wings, and, when the butterfly was dry and stuck in his collection, it looked as if it would fly away at the least disturbance. Not so with me. I could never get the wings to stay in the correct position without tearing them, or rubbing off half the coloured scales. Moreover, I could seldom make the wings spread out the same on both sides. The effect of all this was that my collection was a lot of transparent, tattered, unidentifiable little bodies, which always managed to look as if someone had trodden on them.

Father took a lively interest in Dick's collection and would get as excited as anyone over some rare specimen. He had his own butterfly net, which he jealously guarded, and liked to organize family expeditions to various forests or hills in the neighbourhood, where Dick told him that the butterflies were likely to be different from those on the open savannah of the farm. We all joined in enthusiastically and, as far as I was concerned, those trips were visits to paradise, especially when we went to a forest.

By far the best of the forests within reach of Porgies was called Kabrass, a great stretch of virgin jungle in the Kavirondo Reserve, not far from Lake Victoria. A visit to Kabrass meant a journey of two or three hours, but we prepared for it with the care and excitement of an expedition up the Nile. The old box-bodied Chevrolet was packed the night before with food, rugs and all the gear we needed for catching and keeping butterflies. Not only nets, killing bottles and 'flat fifty' cigarette tins full of the little envelopes for storing the specimens, but breeding cages, hooks and hatchets for pulling down and cutting off succulent branches of food plants. And bait.

Bait included almost anything unwholesome and smelly that Dick thought might be appetizing to butterflies. He had done quite a bit of research on this and came up with some truly hideous offerings. Different butterflies, he found, were turned on by different things, the only common factor being that they all liked their food high. And Dick tried to cater for every taste. Rotten fish, fermented fruit, scraped-up droppings of dogs, cats and chickens, blended together with molasses and a drop of Guinness – the list was comprehensive. All this was carefully slopped into jars, labelled and packed into the car. Of course, I tried my hand at it too and let my imagination fly. But butterflies can be selective and usually my efforts were too disgusting even for them. We set off an hour or so before dawn, so as to have a full day in the forest. Or so it was said. I suspect, though, that that was not the only reason. That bait got pretty friendly in the hot sun.

Dawn in the tropics is as quick and dramatic as sunset. At half-past five it is dark and at six the sun sails up over the horizon and the world is suddenly thrown into fierce relief. Long black shadows stride away from the smallest bush and the light is clear and brilliant. The day wastes no time in getting underway.

If there were no hitches like a puncture, or one of us being sick, we would reach Kabrass Forest just as the sun came up.

The car breasted a rise, and there was the forest, a dark band of trees across the road. As we got closer there appeared an even darker patch, like the entrance to a tunnel, where the road entered the trees.

The first sight of that tunnel always made my heart beat faster. There was something mysterious and a little bit frightening about the gaping mouth of the forest in the early dawn. As you entered it the road dipped quite sharply and the change of light, to say nothing of atmosphere, was very abrupt. The family teased me about it. As we came up to it everyone started a low murmur, rather in the manner of a cricket crowd urging on their favourite fast bowler as he races up to the wicket. I joined in – but my heart was always in my mouth.

Suddenly, with a shout, we plunged into a lovely dark green world. The tops of the trees, seemingly miles above us, would sway excitedly as if in a sudden wind, as a troop of monkeys made off at our approach. Great noisy hornbills would honk through the forest, their voices echoing all round us, and clouds of butterflies rose from the muddy culverts at the side of the road. Father would stop the car at our favourite picnic spot and, for a moment, we all sat awestruck in the cathedral-like gloom, listening to the myriad sounds of the magic place.

One thing Dick was adamant about was that we should all contain our morning bowel movements till we reached the forest. He would pompously explain – he was of the age when exact terminology took precedence over wit – that human faeces were most attractive to the males of the more exotic types of butterfly. Apparently, the females, wise little things, preferred the fermented fruit. By that stage of the morning no-one could blame them.

So, once we had unpacked the car and had had breakfast, everybody's first task – first thought, too, in most cases – was to disappear, under Dick's expert generalship, with little bits of paper, to various strategic spots to do our duty. And woe betide any of us if we left our little offerings where they could not be reached – or, at least, easily 'netted'.

While my mother and the girls sorted out the camp, Father, Dick and I set out all the different bits of bait in suitable places, nailing fish heads to trees and smearing the whole noisome delicatessen onto branches, logs and roadside locations. We also looked out for, and marked, any ready-made delights, such as leopard droppings, oozing bits of sap, or rotting fruit under a forest tree.

I was not a very adventurous little boy, for I never strayed far from the road on these expeditions. The forest growth was thick and jungly and grew well over my head. It would be so easy to get lost. Besides, there were all sorts of hazards underfoot and, as I never wore shoes, I was chary about where I trod. Creeping things that bit were never far from my thoughts for, wherever I went, I was always followed by my mother's injunction to 'watch out for snakes'. It must have been a constant anxiety to her to have all of us scantily shod children crashing about among the trees.

Actually, thorns were much more of a menace than snakes, for snakes on the whole made off at the approach of clumsy humans. Thorns, however, stay put, and Africa is full of thorns. Seldom a day passed without a session with the needle to dig them out of my feet. And not only thorns. Jiggers, too, were an ever-present threat. These little horrors, minute insects about the size of a flea (in fact, I believe they are a sort of flea), have a fondness for getting under toenails, burrowing under the soft skin there and laying a tiny sac of eggs. All one is aware of at first is a tiresome itch, but, unless the egg sac is removed, the eggs hatch out into lots of little jiggers who burrow a bit further in and lay eggs of their own. And so on. We once saw an African whose leg had been eaten halfway up his calf by a whole dynasty of jiggers.

The important thing was to get the sac out intact, for, if it was broken, the eggs were so small and numerous it was almost impossible to clear them all out. Just one left inside could start the whole family tree growing again. So my toes were regularly examined and, if a jigger was discovered, I was in for a hard time. There are some advantages, I suppose, in wearing shoes.

But, to get back to thorns. There was one particular bush in the forest which we all regarded with the greatest respect. We called it the wait-a-bit thorn. It was a pretty little bush, like a very delicate briar. But the thorns were long and severely hooked and very sharp. If you caught your clothes in it you were very soon entangled, because the movement needed to get one hooked thorn from a sleeve invariably resulted in several more catching bits of you or your clothing. It could be quite alarming to get caught by a wait-a-bit when out of earshot of the others because, unless you were to do yourself nasty damage, you needed help to get disentangled. There was one occasion – I think it was actually in Kabrass – when Father had thought he had chosen a perfect spot to lay his treasure for the gentlemen butterflies. As he tried to stand to pull up his trousers, he gave a yell of alarm. Rushing to the spot, fearing that he had at least roused a sleeping leopard, we found him, his pants round his ankles and swearing terribly, wrapped in the loving embrace of a wait-a-bit. It was some time before he saw the funny side.

There was another tree in the forest which produced the most beautiful rich brown velvet seed pods. I always found these a temptation – or a challenge, I can't imagine why. I should have known better, for I always came off second best. The merest touch of these lovely soft things produced an extremely painful rash. There were gorgeous hairy caterpillars, too, looking like doll's house broom-heads. They had the same effect.

In this connection, I developed a short-lived habit of sniffing any flower that came my way. The discovery of flower scents is exciting and heady; African wild flowers are nearly all highly scented, though not all the scents are pleasant. It was fun, all the same, to find out. But my habit was smartly broken one day in Kabrass when I buried my face into a bunch of some sort of exotic stinging nettle. I would not advise anyone to try this. My nose felt as if it were full of very angry bees and my long-suffering mother had to pour most of the picnic milk into my nostrils to cool them off.

But, in spite of the dangers and pitfalls (probably partly

because of them), Kabrass Forest always held a special magic for me. The enormous trees, arching overhead like the tracery of some great abbey, stirring and rustling, filtering the sunlight through a million leaves, filled me with awe. It was like looking at unexplored territory; no-one had ventured up into those delicate, swaying branches where a whole strange life went on, independent of and more exciting than life on the ground. Not only were there clans of monkeys, moving fast and surely along their own mysterious highways, but there were great big raucous birds, little shrill brilliant ones, dun-coloured, silent secretive ones; and, of course, a host of lizards, snakes and squirrel-like animals that watched you warily, or skittered hurriedly round to the leeward side of the tree trunks.

But, above all, there were the butterflies. They never let us down.

The forest butterflies were more exciting than the ones we knew on the farm. There were many more here, for one thing, always competing for the best bits of food. They rose in clouds from muddy patches or from flowering shrubs; more often than not, though, when settled on one of the baits, they were so intent on their pungent meal that they could be picked off like fruit, or closely examined to see if they were worth picking off. That is, if one cared to get that close to their dinner. They also liked to gather in places where a patch of sunlight filtered through the trees. They were of all shapes and sizes: little brown speckled fritillaries; great long-tailed floppy papilios; scarlet, blue or iridescent little beauties; and the fierce, powerful, purposeful bullies from the high branches who sometimes took time off to chase their frailer brethren. Then, in the darker, danker parts of the forest, there were huge slow mother-of-pearl butterflies and dark glowing creatures that looked like dead leaves until they opened their wings and flew, when they would gleam like blue, green or mauve shadows. These liked to roost in the culverts under the road where they gathered in hundreds, looking like old cobwebs as they hung in clusters in the half-light.

It was tacitly understood that Dick, the expert, had first go at any bait or bush, for he was extremely selective and never took a specimen if he did not need it for his collection. I, on the other hand, rushed about catching anything I could put my net to, squashing or breaking more than ever I collected. Dick often came to the forest to find one particular butterfly and sometimes spent the whole day sitting beside a particular bait or known food plant, watching behaviour, or waiting for the creature to come down to his lure from the tops of the trees. When it arrived he moved silently, making sure his shadow did not fall across it, and picked it off the bait with such delicacy that he did not disturb a single scale. He squeezed it gently to force its wings open, but without injuring it; if it was not what he was after he always released it, raising his hand after it in a gentle gesture of farewell. But, if it was the one he had been waiting for, he would either squeeze the life out of it between thumb and forefinger, or pop it into his cyanide killing bottle, where it flopped about for a few moments, before it collapsed and died, stupefied by the fumes.

He then carefully placed it in one of his paper envelopes and stored it in a cigarette tin, to be dealt with when he got home.

On one of these Kabrass expeditions I discovered, to my horror, that I had left my net behind. I was inconsolable. The day was ruined. Dick had not brought a spare and Father said he could not possibly lend his – it was too precious, and too heavy for me, anyway. I must have worked myself up into a real lather, for my mother's solution was, by any token, drastic. She removed her bloomers, cut them in half, and sewed up a makeshift net for me out of one voluminous knicker leg. It was quite unsuitable, for it was made of heavy green satin and I do not think I caught anything with it, but at least I was equipped and stopped being a nuisance. It was a measure of our poverty at the time that I believe she sewed the legs back together again when we got home and continued to wear those pants for some time.

As the shadows began to lengthen, we hurriedly packed up and piled into the car for the journey home. It was always dark long before we got there and this was something else I loved. The headlamps of the car picked up all sorts of night creatures using the road as they set about their night's hunting. Jackals, hyenas, rabbits and all sorts of foxes and cats and smaller, weasel-like animals stared, transfixed, into the blinding glare. Father would slow down and bang the car door with the flat of his hand to break their trance. Even then whatever it was would run dottily along the road in front, lurching from side to side, as if the beam of light were a tunnel from which it could not escape. 'Come on, you silly little blighters,' Father would shout, his head poking out of the window, and we would all boo at it, till the terrified creature found a friendly shadow through which it could dart to safety.

Sometimes a large floppy moth, big as a small bird, lumbered suicidally into the headlights. Then Dick always wanted to stop and investigate, but it had usually buried itself messily into the radiator, together with a million other victims.

Then it was home to mugs of condensed milk and hot water laced with whisky, all of us tumbling sleepily and still dirty into bed under our mosquito nets. Even so, my mother never missed out on our prayers – if such they could be called. They never varied. A short prayer, which started, 'Pray God' – the rest of which I have lost – and some mumbled verse of a hymn:

Jesus, tender Shepherd, hear me,
Bless thy little lamb tonight,
Through the darkness be thou near me [a high note here]
Keep me safe till morning light,
AAA – men.

IV

I T WAS NOT ONLY ENGLAND THAT WAS STRANGE TO ME when
I found myself at Allesley Rectory; religiously, too, I was an
unmarked page, or very nearly so. Apart from my mother's
nightly prayer routine, my experience of anything to do with
God was sketchy indeed. I remember crying copiously at a
scratchy recording of Clara Butt singing the aria 'He was
despised and rejected' from Handel's *Messiah*, though no-one
ever told me why it was so sad. Occasionally we were visited
by a peripatetic clergyman called Tyree who turned up
unexpectedly at the farm in a tiny Ford two-seater with a
dicky at the back. He patted our heads and held a sort of
service round the dining-room table, which I did not understand and at which we all tried not to giggle, much to my
mother's embarrassment. Mr Tyree was as small as his car,
with fair hair and a face burnt permanently red by the sun. He
had an odd sing-song delivery which reduced my sisters to
paroxysms, so of course I joined in, though I could not quite
see why; he just seemed boring to me. Poor man! If all his
pastoral visits were like that, his life must have been a trial to

him. My mother was grateful to him for coming, but Father said he was a silly arse. I cannot think that spiritually we got much out of these visits.

So I was surprised to find that the life of a Church of England rector and his family was as normal as anyone else's. Family prayers that first morning was something of a facer, though, and was one of my first lessons in instant adaptation.

We sat round in a circle in my uncle's study: the rector himself, my Aunt Ailie and Bobby and the staff – Nellie Britain, the cook, and her tarty, teenage daughter, Peggy; old Annie Coleman, the superannuated Nannie, blind and strict and devout; and Ivy, the maid, in black with a cap rammed right down over her resentful eyebrows. The rector read a piece of scripture and, if my memory does not fail me, we wavered through a hymn, led by the hooting mezzo of my aunt. Then we turned round and knelt at our chairs, our behinds facing the middle, staring through the backs like animals through the bars of a cage, while the rector said a few prayers. One or other of us was asked to pronounce the grace at the end.

I was introduced to the staff as Master Walter. Ivy was aloof and respectful, and Peggy immediately summed me up as too young for interest. Annie I had met the night before. I was a little alarmed by her – she seemed very strict and full of nannyish wise saws. And, blind she may have been, but she could spot a missing button at fifty yards. Of course, when I got to know her, she was a friend and an ally always. She was totally unsentimental, but seemed to know instinctively what a big world it all seemed to me.

But Nellie became an instant friend. Big and jolly with a shiny face and cosy BO that only seemed to make her more human, she presided over the part of the house through the green baize door (literally) with a cheerful authority that extended to everyone but Peggy, who was a flouncing law unto herself. Nellie was an indifferent cook; her apple pies were basins of floating bullets covered with a lid of concrete. But nobody seemed to mind and for years I thought that that was what apple pies were supposed to be like. I found it difficult to grasp that white people could have white servants. Where I came from all servants were black. Nellie made the transition easier for me because, although she called Ailie 'M'm' and took her daily orders from her, there was nothing servile or distant about her. She knew her position in the household, and was everyone's friend. Bobby taught me to go into the kitchen if I felt peckish, because Nellie always had a titbit of something or other.

My cousin, Sue, I had yet to meet and it was a prospect I viewed with some trepidation. She was not only a girl – well, that was all right; I knew about sisters – but Susan was almost my contemporary: I was trespassing on her emotional territory. African girls, too, I knew about, but I had no experience of how to cope with a white girl of my own age. Grown-ups were much easier to deal with. Still, our meeting was not to be for three weeks when the schools broke up for Christmas, so I could postpone that problem. I had, after all, plenty of others to face.

Bobby went back to Bradfield for the last weeks of term and

I was left in sole occupancy of the bedroom at the far end of the house, where the Virginia creeper grew right up to the window, and the birds that roosted in it sounded just like burglars stealthily climbing towards me. I did not dare to tell anyone. I had come from Africa, full of wild beasts and fierce black men. This was England – cosy, safe, cushiony England. There couldn't be anything to be afraid of, could there? But I lay petrified in that room, night after night, wondering if I would have time to find a weapon to hit the intruder with before he got me.

I have never really grown out of my fear of the dark. It is not so bad if I am dressed and on the move; but lying in bed listening, I am a crab out of its shell, and the harder I listen, the louder becomes the pounding of my own pulse in my ears. This means that I am missing the stealthy footfall, or the tiny creak of a floorboard. Which makes it worse. Grown-ups can never understand this. 'You're quite safe – we're here.' But they're not: they are in another room. Minding anything but my business. Or asleep, which is even more undermining.

It was the Yellow Cat which started it, though of course the African night has never been exactly tranquil, and I was always uneasy if I woke in the middle of the night, when the whole world was croaking or whistling, scratching or howling away. The calmness of adults at such times was beyond belief. Lying awake in the dark trying to identify the murderer's step or the lion's grunt above the contented snoring of oblivious parents is what is being kept warm for me in Purgatory.

The regular night sounds of Porgies were all this, and more. Frogs and crickets and mice, the sudden whirr of a nightjar, and the mocking, wild, ventriloquist's 'Cooooloooeeeooo' of the spotted hyena, could set my scalp on the crawl. Just before dawn there came the eerie foghorn booming of the ground hornbill, and one particular bird sang loud and sudden just before the sun rose. I got up one morning, skin prickling at my own daring, to try and get a look at it, but I saw no more than a grey blur as it disappeared into the mango tree at the top of the garden. I was not quite brave enough to follow it – after all, it was still almost dark, and there might be some great beast that had had a poor night's hunting, and would just fancy a light breakfast of small boy. I told Dick about this bird; he was the expert, after all. But Dick was a heavy sleeper, an insensitive adult; he had never heard it, and said I was making it up. All night, though, jackals barked, owls groaned and screamed, and occasionally there came the gentlemanly cough of a leopard, prowling round the *boma* in the hope that one of the dogs was loose.

But the sound that has always made my spit dry up and breathing become an effort, is the mating call of the domestic tom-cat, out on the tiles in the small hours. I lie there very still, hoping that he will soon get what he is after and shut up, and I have no doubt at all that the cause of this singling out was the Yellow Cat. I give him capitals because, for about a century when I was nearly seven, he claimed a lot of my attention during the day, and all of it at night.

The Yellow Cat was an enormous ginger tom who spent his

days holed up in the grain store, a thatched rondavel about fifty yards from the house. If I opened the door in the middle of the day and peeped inside, it was a delicious moment of terror to catch the gleam of two green eyes blazing at me from the dark interior. With my heart in my throat I would make a sudden clatter, and the Yellow Cat would scramble out between the walls and the roof, making my hair stand on end, and streak away towards the bush. I sometimes had time intrepidly to throw a stone after him, and he always stopped and looked back pityingly before he disappeared. He knew I was no match for him and so did I. But I had to keep my end up, for I was mortally afraid of him.

Where he came from nobody knew. He must have been descended from someone's pet, for some atavistic message kept him always near the house. But he was as wild as the servals that occasionally left a mess of bloody feathers to explain the loss of another hen from my mother's brood. Father often read us Kipling's story of 'The Cat That Walked by Itself', and I loved it because I found it scary. That cat, I was certain, was yellow.

It did not occur to any of us to try and tame the Yellow Cat, and I doubt if we could have succeeded if we had tried. I cannot think that there was anything benign about him. But he was magnificent.

Our old grey moggy was the cause of the trouble. She was fat, sleek, lazy and fecund, and produced litters of kittens as often as nature allowed. Grey kittens, tabby, black, white, every sort of kitten trooped from her ample frame. Nobody wanted them, so they had to be destroyed. For some reason, unwanted kittens were always drowned in a bucket of water, a slow and macabre job that was left to poor old Dick. My mother refused to think about it; the girls were upset by it; but I found it ghoulishly fascinating. No-one asked the old grey cat what she thought, but it never deterred her from producing more sacrificial litters.

The Yellow Cat, however, had a quicker method.

The regular litter had appeared, as usual, behind a pile of firewood in the kitchen, where it squirmed and squeaked in a heaving mass as the kittens tugged at the belly of their purring parent. One morning my mother got up to make the tea, and found the old cat disturbed and restless, trying to move her babies to another nest.

Investigating, she found that out of a litter of half a dozen, three had had their throats neatly torn out. Dick was most intrigued by this, and discovered that all the murdered kittens were toms; the survivors were female. At that stage nobody guessed who the culprit might be; the Yellow Cat was just one of a host of feral cats which hung around the farm. But whoever had done it was not planning on having any rivals about the place.

Then the cat produced another litter – this time all ginger, so paternity was not much in doubt. They were very beautiful, and the family decided to keep them. They were apportioned between us with much argument and not a few tears. Not as many as there were a few mornings later, when we found half the litter dead, with their throats torn out.

This seemed to point to a change in the pattern. Ginger cats, we had been told, were always toms – the female equivalent is the tortoiseshell. So the old boy had got it wrong for once. Dick, the expert on these matters, investigated again, just to prove the point.

The three ginger survivors were females.

For some reason, this discovery turned the Yellow Cat into a sinister kind of threat, and the rest of the family began to take him seriously. This was a relief to me, for I had been taking him seriously for some time.

My sister, Tricia, and I, as the youngest, always had our bath together and we had the habit afterwards of squatting round the hurricane lamp on the floor of our bedroom, playing or talking and letting the warm night air dry us before getting into our pyjamas. The window of the room was quite high up in the wall – or it seemed high to me – and outside the window, on the back verandah, sacks of coffee were piled right up to it. One night, as we squatted drying, I glanced up at a movement and saw a large yellow furry face at the window. I will always swear it was making faces at me. I let out a yell of terror, and ran, stark naked, into the dining room, where the rest of the family were having supper. The alarm was raised. I claimed that it was a human face, all covered with fur.

Father and Dick took out their guns and went on a search, but nothing was found. Could it have been one of the *shamba* boys doing a peeping Tom? No, I said. It was furry – and yellow. Everyone relaxed – except me. It must have been my old friend, they said, and teased me about it. What I could not possibly explain was that this only made it worse: if it was the cat, how could I now make anyone take seriously my belief that it had been pulling faces at me?

After this I was so frightened of the dark that my little bed was moved into my parents' room, and a fresh hook screwed into the ceiling from which to hang my mosquito net. This was something of a comfort, but it had its disadvantages. For one thing, they came to bed so late and when, finally, they did, I would sometimes lie awake, listening intently to the night, trying to filter each tiny sound through Father's happy snores. It was simply incredible to me that anyone could be so off-guard when the dark was so fraught with danger.

One night I heard my parents making love. The only thing that could be said for it was that they were at least awake, but, from what they were saying to each other, I could tell that they were not concerning themselves with my problems. They did not even seem to be aware of the hideous dangers lurking in every shadow. All they were doing, as far as I could tell, was thoughtlessly giving away their – and my – position. I was furious; and a bit jealous, too, for I knew what they were doing. When I told my friend Simiu the next day he laughed and said he would have to find someone to share my bed. This seemed the first sensible idea anyone had had recently, but I knew that it could not happen.

Simiu, my little African henchman, and his friends were allowed to sleep with little girls before either reached puberty, after which they were strictly segregated till marriage. For some reason this practice was frowned on by white people, so there was no chance for me. I had a vague idea, from hearsay and boasting, what one was supposed to do with little girls, and it sounded nice. The fact that my mother and father also – and still – found it nice was of only passing interest at that moment of peril.

In fact, Simiu was as good as his word, though I must have been a sad disappointment to him. He called me into one of the native huts in the compound a couple of nights later and, after some whispered instructions, pushed me in and ran off to sit with his friends by the water fire at the back of the house to await events.

It was very dark inside the hut. I stood quite still for a moment in the warm darkness which smelt of woodsmoke and bodies, and wondered what was expected of me. Then I heard a rustle and a soft giggle, and realized that there really was a girl there. My insides lurched in crisis. As my eyes grew accustomed to the dark, I could see a figure huddled under a blanket on the floor. Fascinated and terrified, but with as much composure as my six years could muster, I clambered under the blanket, realizing as I did so that I had no idea who she was. She giggled again.

I had a sketchy idea of what I was supposed to do; at least, I had been told what to say, and Simiu had assured me that the rest would follow from that. The sound of the words of this magic formula have stayed with me always, though my Swahili and Kitosh have long since gone. It sounded like 'Mupé Communyé' which, for all its melting softness, is a bald demand that gets straight to the point. (*Mupé* means give. It does not even incorporate the word for 'please'.)

I suppose that fate was protecting me, but I am afraid that it was sheer funk that made my tongue cleave to the roof of my mouth, for, try as I might, I could not get the words out. Rigid with shyness, still dressed in my khaki shorts and bush jacket, I just lay there, lustful but panicked. I knew how Simiu would scoff if I failed (though what constituted success was not totally clear). And, to make matters worse, the giggles began to take on a note of derision. Knowing that it was now or never, I took a deep breath – and heard my mother calling me into the house for supper. Relief got the better of lust, and I stumbled from the hut and back into the world I knew something about. And I never found out who she was.

So I had no bedfellow to comfort me, and the Yellow Cat was still around.

One night I heard him calling urgently. With skin tingling, it occurred to me that he was actually inside the house. Father snored on; nobody else stirred. The cat called again, much nearer this time. Still no stirring. How could anyone sleep through this?

He called again, and with exquisite terror I realized that he was standing beside my bed, just outside the mosquito net. I have never, before or since, been quite so frightened as I was at that moment. I could taste my fear. How long the cat stayed there I have no idea, but it cannot have been very long, because I know I stopped breathing while he was there, and I

69

am still alive. After what seemed like a year, I heard him call from the kitchen and I became aware that my nails were digging painfully into my palms. I must have fallen asleep at last from sheer exhaustion; but nowhere seemed safe when the Yellow Cat could walk arrogantly and unmolested through the house.

I must have made a nuisance of myself, because finally it was decided that something should be done. Dick built a huge clumsy trap out of wood and wire netting, baited it with a piece of meat, and we waited. Each morning we would rush out to see what had been captured, I in my pyjamas, making sure I was not alone. Usually the bait was gone and the trap empty, which could have been anything from mice to ants; sometimes it waited untouched and ignored. And once a small angry animal like a weasel was spitting and cursing through the wire. But not the Yellow Cat.

Then Dick had a success, which at least showed that his trap worked. I had just been put to bed, the family were having supper, and my nightly vigil was underway, when there was an appalling noise from the direction of the trap. Triumphantly we all rushed out with torches and guns.

In the trap was an enormous cat, spitting and snarling, eyes blazing furiously at the indignity of his capture. But he was not yellow. He was black and white and had only one and a half ears to pin back at us. He was a fearsome sight, but he seemed almost cosy to me. It did not save him, though; he was dispatched with the casual callousness that was natural to us all. A bullet through the head, and thrown out for the scavengers. Maybe I am being unjust to my father and brother; perhaps he was buried – I do not remember. But animal life was always cheap in those days.

Two or three more cats suffered the same fate in Dick's trap. But not the Yellow Cat. He knew better.

Perhaps if I had not been so upset by him, he might have been left to live out his natural span. But I think my mother noticed the rings of sleeplessness under my eyes. At any rate, my father decided on drastic action. It was stupid, and it was cruel, and I have never understood why the cat was not simply shot. Perhaps my father had the idea of a bit of sport.

He discovered from me that the Yellow Cat always holed out in the grain store. So he and Dick and I and several of the *shamba* boys, having blocked up all possible exits, surrounded the hut armed with sticks, put the old dog Porge inside, and shut the door. A noisy, brutal and short battle took place inside and then, silence, except for a soft whine. We opened the door. Porge came blinking out into the sunlight, her muzzle bloody and a large scratch down her nose.

Dick and some boys went inside, and emerged in a moment amid excited chatter and flung to the ground an enormous yellow corpse. It was immediately covered with flies.

A hole was dug in the garden and the body thrown in. Father called me over.

'There he is, old man. All over now.'

I looked down into the grave. Green eyes stared up at me

unblinking, and the hairs on my neck stirred. I did not stop long.

The sequel was sad, but predictable. Within two weeks Porge had killed all three ginger kittens. On the assumption, I suppose, that yellow cats were fair game.

V

ONCE AGAIN, I WAS ON A TRAIN WITH DUFF WHO HAD come from Leamington to collect me. This time we were on our way to London to get me registered for Christ's Hospital at the school offices and then on to Horsham to see the school itself. It was only about a week since I had arrived at Allesley and events were still like great mattresses, pressing in on me. And it was cold. Always, it seemed, ears and nose, fingers and toes were distracted with cold. English people did not seem to notice the cold, or stamped about cheerfully, with clouds of steam coming from their mouths as they spoke. Duff wore mittens, which seemed pointless to me; why leave your fingers exposed when you could cover them completely with proper gloves? Her nose was permanently pink and shiny and she peered cheerfully through her thick spectacles. She was the only one who said she thought I was 'brave'. I did not quite know what she meant. I was just surviving. Bravery did not come into it.

Back in the hullabaloo of London, I was relieved that Duff seemed to know what she was doing. To me it was all totally confusing, with cars and people and buses and horses going every which way, and much too fast. But Duff led me confidently to the underground and in no time we were at Tower Hill.

At the school offices in Great Tower Street we were ushered into a large room with high vaulted windows. We were the only ones. It appeared that all the other boys of the next intake had already been seen, so it all seemed a bit uncertain and irregular. However, the clerk of the school was kindly and checked my name off against a long list. And that was all. We were let out again.

Everything was very tall; tall buildings towering over dark narrow streets which echoed to the sounds of tall buses and the clopping of tall dray horses. The pavements seemed to be permanently damp and slippery. Duff said it was called 'The City'.

We caught a bus to Victoria and a train to Christ's Hospital. The school must be very big to rate its own station. It was. Enormous expanses of playing fields disappeared into the mist and a line of tall red-brick buildings, each the same as its neighbour, stretched from one side of my vision to the other. These were the houses, we were told, sixteen of them. We saw the quad and big school and the vast dining hall, with its own distinctive smell that was to become so familiar to me and to generations of Blues.

The avenue stretched from one end of the school to the other, giving access to each of the houses. At one end of the avenue was a pair of houses, exactly the same as the others,

74

but separated from the rest. These were the two prep houses and Duff and I were led into the end one – Prep B. We had been met at the station and taken round the school by a tall thin man with a moustache and the biggest Adam's apple I had ever seen which moved up and down as he spoke. This was Mr Willink, the head of Prep B, and he welcomed us kindly and took us over the comfortless building, which seemed to be full of small boys all shouting confidently at each other. The dayroom crammed with long tables and benches; long bleak dormitories with low beige-painted beds, neatly made up and with a settle at each; and changing rooms which seemed to consist of endless rows of hooks festooned with towels and coats and rugger kit. The whole place smelled unmistakeably of school. I tried not to think about it.

I liked Mr Willink immediately. He was kind and made a lot of feeble punning jokes in a strangulated tenor with no lower register. It turned out that he always sang the tenor role in Handel's *Messiah* in big school every year. He sat Duff down with a cup of tea and *The Times* and took me into his study. He put me at a desk with paper and pens and told me to write down the answers to a set of questions which he then handed to me.

I realized that this was some sort of exam and was thoroughly alarmed. I had sat no examination before being awarded the scholarship in Kenya, so I always suspected that I had won it under false pretences. And, here, of course, was the proof. This was the exam I should have taken. Suppose I failed? Would I be sent straight back to Kenya? Back *home*?

Half apprehensive, and half excited, I looked at the paper Mr Willink had given me – and was even more unnerved. The questions were so easy. I thought there must be some sort of catch, though I could not for the life of me see what it was. I looked up at Mr Willink. He was smiling.

'Can you do them?' he asked.

'I think so, sir,' I answered. 'But—'

'You shouldn't find them too hard, I think.'

I finished the paper in half the time allotted. However hard I tried, I could not make it last any longer.

Mr Willink took up my paper and glanced at it. Then he showed me out, where Duff was waiting, trying not to look nervous.

'That's all, Mrs Evans,' he said. 'I think it will be all right. You will be hearing from us.'

I looked at Duff. What did he mean by 'all right'? And who was Mrs Evans? Evans is a common name. Had he got the wrong one? Duff opened her mouth, but Mr Willink went straight on.

'If we hurry, you should be able to catch the four-fifteen,' he said. It sounded like a dismissal. We followed him sheepishly out to his car.

In the train again I looked at Duff. She seemed a trifle put out. 'What is it?' she said.

'The exam was so easy. I'm sure I got it all wrong. Will they send me back to Kenya?'

'Of course not,' said Duff firmly, but her eyes belied her confidence. We were neither of us to know that the test I had sat was merely to discover which form I was to be placed in when I started next term. We returned to Coventry in a state of great uncertainty. It was of course Ailie who hooted with laughter when we told her of our misgivings, and explained what it must have been about. Indeed, in her forthright way she rang up the school the next day and confirmed it.

So I was reprieved – or sentenced? I could not make up my mind. I longed to go back to Africa and to my family; but it would have been an ignominious defeat to have returned without taking part in the great adventure. Besides, it would not have been back to Porgies and Simiu and all my friends. That had gone long since. Even the family had dispersed. Probably, knowing how young they married, most of my old friends would be dispersed too.

Near the house at Porgies, at one side of the main garden, was a huge tree with great branches arching overhead and hanging down almost to the ground, making a wonderful shady marquee from which we had hung ropes and swings and old tyres; a wonderful place to play, out of the fierce overhead tropical sun.

Next to this great tree, so that it was shaded from the worst of the midday sun, Dick had built a large wire-netting cage, for breeding his butterflies. But he found it unsatisfactory. Either the caterpillars got out, or parasitic insects got in and destroyed them.

So he abandoned his big cage and transferred his breeding operations indoors to his bedroom, and the girls began to use it as an aviary. This did not last long either, for invariably some infant bird was left out in a downpour and many a tear was shed – by Dorothy in particular – as she tried to administer the kiss of life to some bloated and drowned fledgling. In the end I acquired it to house my collection of quail. These pretty little birds which like to run along the ground like inverted teacups on wheels used the furrows between the rows of maize as runways. The Africans snared them with two sticks supporting a slip-knot of oxtail hair. Simiu and the others taught me how to do this, but it was easier to rely on the farm boys bringing them up to the house in little wicker cages; I would barter them for a large Golden Syrup tin full of *posho* – the ground mealie meal which was their staple diet.

I built up quite a respectable collection of quail. I usually kept it at about thirty, when my mother would raid it to make quail pie. There seemed to be several types of quail. The commonest was the migratory bird that comes to northern Europe in the summer months, with its beautiful clear etching-like markings; but there were many variants of this and I had one specimen that was almost black with red markings, that I suspect was rare.

The quail were brought to me often from quite distant places, because there was a network of information among the Africans, fed principally by my friend Simiu.

Simiu was the son of one of the *shamba* boys, Agaconya, and I can only assume that my parents had picked him out to keep an eye on me, because we became inseparable friends and went all over the farm together. There had been a previous friend, Wanyonyi, whose job was to lead the ox-team, but the friendship did not last long for some reason; in fact, Wanyonyi became *persona non grata* among our group, and Simiu was careful to keep him at a distance.

Simiu was not only my friend, but my confidant as well and I suspect that, having established him as my bodyguard, my parents found our intimacy something of a worry. After all, to them an African was definitely an inferior being and to find that I would rather be with him than any of our white neighbours' children must have been a little disconcerting.

I remember once my mother 'accidentally' wiped some black shoe polish onto my arm when I was not looking. Some time later she stopped me and asked what the black stain was on my arm. When it would not easily rub off, she said, 'There, you see? That's what happens if you mix too much with the boys. You had better be careful.'

I was thoroughly alarmed and scrubbed my arm till it was sore. When eventually the polish wore off, I challenged my parents and they said they were only teasing. But I was shocked at the deception and realized dimly, even then, how deep the colour prejudice ran.

Nothing, though, made any difference to my affection for Simiu. He was a compact, co-ordinated little boy who must have been three or four years older than me, and he would wait for me outside the house every morning after breakfast. I was the 'bwana *kidogo*', the little master, in the presence of my family; but, once we were out of sight of the house, it was I who became the disciple and Simiu the leader. He taught me how to cut a '*kiboko*', the short throwing stick which they all carried, and I tried to throw it at birds or rabbits as they did, but never achieved anything like sufficient accuracy. (I had a catapult which Father had made for me, with which I was quite proficient, which redressed the balance of power a little – not much, because Simiu was good with it too.) He taught me how to pull thorns out of feet and fingers with a bent piece of dried grass; and how to call the doves down from the trees. He could make a fire and cook a meal anywhere in the woods and he knew which berries were edible.

Together, we explored every part of the farm. He showed me the native paths that led to fords across the river into the reserve; the best pools from which to catch the large black catfish; where to look for the big tortoises; and how far away from a porcupine to stand so as not to get stuck with its quills. He taught me how to lime the bright green pigeons that fed in the wild fig trees. I loved him.

His sister Nafula – or Nuffy, as we called her – was the sort of maid of all work in the house. She was a pretty, precocious little thing, with a mind of her own and a gleaming white quartz pebble decorating a hole in her lower lip. She was everybody's confidante, and made no bones about giving her opinion. She was also the exception to the rule that Africans were not allowed into the house, for she helped to make the beds and do the washing, and was always ready to advise my sisters if they were in difficulties. She and Simiu were permanently in a state of armed neutrality, each jealously guarding their own area of privilege.

But they joined forces in promoting my relationship with Namuhorsi.

I am sure, though, that it started further back than either of them. Through the rolling clouds of early memory I knew a lap; a dark brown fragrant skin; a smile above me that caught my heart. I am on that lap, for some reason, and there are several little girls, and talk, and laughter; and we are sitting in a nest among the mealies in Father's big barn.

I cannot think why that special lap, that skin, that smile, should be the one that stirs my memory; I must have known dozens of similar ones. My sisters used me as a sort of multi-purpose doll, to be dressed and undressed and passed round; swaddled and cuddled and meddled with by anyone who wanted a go at me. But that lap, that skin, that smile, stayed with me – stays with me still – linked with the name, Namuhorsi. Only a few years ago I was sitting in a tube train in London. I looked up and noticed opposite me a young black girl. She had bare arms, and her skin had a sheen that carried me back over fifty years. It was only a momentary reaction, the girl did not look up from her book, and I got out at the next station. But, for the next quarter-hour, I walked in a daze of memory, thinking of a name I had not thought about for decades, Namuhorsi.

Porgies was supplied with many basic necessaries – eggs, milk, chickens and the occasional sheep for slaughtering – from the local African *shambas*. When my mother bought eggs, she always put them first in a bowl of water. If they sank to the bottom, it meant that they were at least wholesome (though possibly fertilized – an unavoidable risk). But, if they floated to the top, this meant that gases had begun to form inside the shell, and the eggs were bad. This was a simple precaution, not resented by the Africans; it was a fair cop. If they could get away with selling the memsahib rotten eggs, then the memsahib had no-one to blame but herself. The same applied to milk. If she did not test the milk with a hydrometer for added water, then more fool her.

And so the milk would arrive every morning, usually in old beer bottles with banana-leaf stoppers, and it was tested as a matter of course. If it had been supplemented by a gill or two from the local stream, the hydrometer would float high above the surface of the liquid, and the milkmaid would be sent home with a flea in her ear.

For the milk was brought to the farm by the daughters of the *shambas* – young, lithe, singing girls, their young bodies moving smoothly under their usually rather grubby dresses or *kikois* (a sort of sarong). Sometimes they wore nothing at all but a string of beads. They carried their loads on their heads, so their movements were stately, and their carriage upright.

One of these milkmaids was Namuhorsi. I caught a glimpse of her most days, and she would smile her wonderful smile, but we seldom spoke. In fact, our meetings were infrequent and unsatisfactory. This was where Simiu and Nuffy came in. They would carefully engineer elaborate 'chance' meetings, but I was always too shy and tongue-tied to do anything about it – though I cannot imagine what I could have done anyway, however confident I might have been. But Namuhorsi never scoffed; she smiled her smile, and went her way, leaving me yearning for I knew not what.

Once I was having a bathe in a river pool on the edge of the reserve. I was up to my waist in the water, when I suddenly became aware that she was under a tree, looking at me. Simiu, who had been bathing with me, all at once was not there. We were alone. We stared at each other. She beckoned me to come out, but I could not. I simply crouched lower in the water and grinned sheepishly, shaking my head. We stayed like that for some time, until finally she smiled again – sadly perhaps? – and slipped away through the trees. Simiu thought I was daft.

Our final meeting was more dramatic. Simiu told me that Namuhorsi was at the bottom of the garden and wanted to see me. I nearly funked it, but Simiu was insistent.

So I made my way down beyond the bananas, and there she was, waiting for me, calm and beautiful. I cannot describe her, for she was for me a sensation rather than a vision. But I suppose she must have been about thirteen, a year or so older than my sister, Tricia. I was all of seven.

She put her arm round me, and we started to walk down the long straight path that led to the coffee plantation, and beyond that to the native reserve. I was emboldened to put my arm round her waist. If I stretched up a bit, I could reach her breast. She did not seem to mind, so I clung on. I cannot imagine that she enjoyed it, but I thought it very sophisticated.

Then she told me that I would not be seeing her again, for she was to be sold in marriage. The bride-price for her would have been at least five cows and several drums of *tembo*, the local African beer. She was a woman, now that she had reached puberty, and her father could no longer afford to keep her. Besides, she was a saleable commodity.

All this I knew, but I could not accept it. I asked her to marry me instead. She did not laugh at me, but explained how impossible that was. I cried, and begged, clinging there to her breast as we wove down the path. No-one else was about, but I would not have cared if there had been. She was always kind; I remember her gentleness with me. But she was also quite firm. She did not particularly want to get married; it would mean the beginning of a life of drudgery and childbearing. But there was nothing she could do about it. I cried and clung, but finally gave up. We said goodbye, and I watched her stately back disappear into the dusk. I dried my tears and made my way home. I never saw her again.

I never knew how much older Simiu was than I, but he must have been about twelve at this time. I knew, though I did not understand what it meant, that dreaded school was looming somewhere ahead for me. I also knew that, with the onset of manhood, which came early for African boys, it would not be long before Simiu would have to put away childish things – like me.

I tried not to think about it, but knew that the great ceremony of circumcision was near at hand, because sometimes Simiu would not be available to come out shooting or climbing trees or catching birds with me. He was away in the reserve, undergoing some sort of instruction course. Learning religious and tribal responsibilities, I suppose.

So our endless, idyllic playing days were beginning to break up, and Simiu's life became full of secrets he was not allowed to share, and there were disdainful refusals to join in our old games and fun.

But then it was realized by Simiu and his group that I was already circumcised, and they said I could possibly be allowed to come and watch the ceremony when the great day arrived. I was taken to Simiu's father, Agaconya, and my little acorn was shown to him. He laughed and said that, as I was already a man, like him, he would tell the priests, and they would allow me to be there.

What excuse I gave to my parents for being out all day I cannot remember, but it was not an unusual thing to happen, so I was given some sort of picnic, warned not to walk in the long grass, and set off early in the morning into the reserve by myself to find my friends. It was easy to find the procession – there was a great racket going on. But, by now, my friends were segregated, and I could not get near them. I knew where they were, because they were at the centre of the procession, with their heads shaven, dressed in white, their faces white like clowns.

I had caught up with the procession near the Kamakoya River on the edge of the farm. Bells were ringing and strange chants being sung. The old men were dancing and leaping about, displaying their circumcised parts proudly, and going through elaborate, but basic, routines. It seemed that the whole tribe was there dressed in their best clothes, and all *en fête*, singing and dancing. Every now and then the procession would stop, and one of the elders, or a priest, would climb into the branches of a tree and harangue his congregation in a sort of wild chant in a rhythmical pattern which drew forth answering cries from the assembled men and boys. Only the circumcised male members of the tribe could be there. The women and children were banned. I felt very proud to be there, but still an outsider, and was ready to be sent home at any moment. However, one of the men who knew me kept an eye on me and whenever my presence was questioned by a stranger – 'What is this *m'zungu* doing here?' – he answered that I had been made a man many years ago by my parents. Once I was ordered to lower my trousers to prove the fact. I was very scared, for the old man who had challenged me was fierce, daubed with mud and ochre, and dressed in a leopard skin. But my tiny member seemed to be a sufficient passport, for his face cracked into a grin and I was allowed to stay, though I kept to the back of the crowd.

Occasionally I caught a glimpse of my friends beyond the heads of the men, but I could not recognize anyone, because their faces had been plastered with thick clay and they all looked alike behind these masks.

The procession seemed to be endless. I suppose they had to come near the *boma* of each of the candidates, for we trekked from one gathering place to another, from one end of the reserve to another, and at each place the same halt would be made. Someone climbed up a tree, and the harangue and response would be repeated. I did not understand a word of it, because, although my kitchen Swahili was better than my English and I had a decent working knowledge of the local patois, the involved language of these sermons was beyond me. I suppose they were exhortations to be manly and upright, honest and potent. Certainly potency came high on the agenda, for everywhere I looked, private parts seemed to be jiggled about like tassles on a stripper.

Finally, as the sun declined towards the west and the shadows began to lengthen on the ground, we came to a pool entirely surrounded by trees. It must have been a sacred place because, in all our exploration of the farm and the reserve, I had never come across it before, and Simiu had never mentioned it. Father must have known about it; it would have been a perfect place for washing coffee beans, but he had not been near it. The odd thing was that I looked for it later, but could never find it.

At this point I was not allowed to be present, for all my potential manhood, but Simiu told me about it. What took place explained the dried clay masks.

One by one they were led to the edge of the pool, where the witch-doctor-priest awaited the candidates, armed with a sharp knife and a specially grown long thumbnail. By this time the clay masks had dried to a hard cake on the boys' faces. As each candidate came forward, his robe was whisked off and the priest grasped the foreskin with his long thumbnail and pulled it towards him. With the knife he deftly snipped off the skin, whereupon a poultice of healing leaves – apparently some sort of nettle – was slapped on the wounded penis, tied on firmly, and the lad was then plunged into the pool up to his neck. If, during this procedure, he so much as winced, the clay on his face would crack and reveal his cowardice, and he would be disgraced.

After a deal more chanting and celebration, the procession moved off again deep into the reserve, for a night of drinking and feasting, and goodness knows what else. But by this time dusk was beginning to fall and I knew that in half an hour it would be dark. I was tired and bewildered. My friends seemed to be very far away from me, spiritually as well as physically. I could not have explained it to anyone, but I felt alone and alienated. Things would never be the same again. What was more, I knew that I could not have been strong enough to go through all that without so much as a small grimace, and I was missing the warmth and comfort of home. Anyway, I was not allowed to be away from the house after dark by myself. So I jogged home, in a mixture of sadness and relief, to a bath and supper.

I did not see Simiu again for some days and, when finally I did see him coming towards the house, he was surrounded by his circumcision group, and different. Their faces were shining with pride and I went to meet them, rather awestruck and diffident. One of their number, I noticed, was following some hundred or so yards behind, completely ignored by the others.

Simiu tried to be superior, but he was too excited, and was soon giving me a vivid, and no doubt exaggerated, account of their experiences. When I asked what Waluchio was doing all by himself, they turned as if they had not seen him there before and, with a lot of shouting and abuse, they picked up sticks and stones and threw them at him. He ran off out of range, but did not go away.

Poor lad, he had nowhere to go. The boys told me that during the ceremony he, alone of all of them, had winced and cried out, and his clay mask had cracked. As a result, they would have nothing to do with him and neither would his family. He was an outcast, like a wounded animal turned out of the pack. It was not a permanent sentence; eventually he would be allowed back into the fold; but while it lasted his exclusion was total. His presence represented bad luck. My sense of compassion may have given me a nudge, but it was no more than that, for, though I do not believe I actually threw things at him, I wanted to be part of the gang, and, like them, pretended that he was not there.

I felt very proud and grown-up to have been permitted to be part of their great day. My friends naturally assumed that I had undergone a similar ordeal in the past (though most of them had known me since I was a baby) and, while I did not actually say that I had, I did not deny it either, for I very much wanted still to belong to the group and I felt certain that I could not have done so had I explained how and when I had been circumcised – not that I had any very clear picture, but an instinct told me that it would not have been enough. And I could not possibly ask my parents, anything to do with sex was simply not discussed, and the thought of going into an elaborate explanation of Simiu's circumcision made me go pale with horror. Any information I had gleaned had been either from my African friends or from my sister Tricia; and her knowledge, I suspect, was even less exhaustive than mine. To walk through that kind of minefield with my mother was out of the question.

At all events, I realized that, by exercising a deviousness of which I am surprised that I was capable, I was still regarded as a member of the club and, though Simiu from that moment tended to scoff at the games we used to play, I could, by doing my own share of scoffing and by demonstrating my disdain of Waluchio, still share his life.

In order that their circumcised penises might heal and be proper weapons for their manhood ahead, Simiu and the others had had instruction in a kind of do-it-yourself sort of treatment which, even to this day, makes my own member recoil in horrified reflex. The boys showed me how they were to break off a piece of thorny cactus leaf which had a long sharp thorn attached to it. With this thorn they were to prick all over the tips of their – well, pricks – in exactly the same way that is done to sloes when making sloe gin. When the poor thing was well and truly punctured, it was smeared all over with the juice of the cactus plant and carefully wrapped in leaves. The only reaction I ever remember them making as they did this was a sharp intake of breath. Either they were very stoical, or their threshold of pain was way higher than mine.

I never knew what the properties of that cactus were, but

they were very effective, for within what seemed a very few days all the boys were completely healed and able to lead a normal life again, whatever that may have entailed. I do not remember any one of them suffering complications.

Poor Waluchio. He did his best to ingratiate himself, but the group would have nothing to do with him, apart from hurling the odd stone at him, and, after a period of hanging about just out of range, he drifted away. I do not remember seeing him again.

VI

THE WINTER CONTINUED COLD AND DANK AND I DEVEL-
oped my first chilblain. But Christmas was coming, and
the preparations, though partly familiar, were in one way
quite new. I had not before come across the religious side of
Christmas. I knew a few of the more familiar carols, but ideas
like Advent – 'Let every heart prepare a throne and every
voice a song,' – were quite new, and I found them intriguing.
My Aunt Ailie gave me careful and interesting instruction
about the Christmas story, and she sang Christmas carols all
day as she went about the house. Bobby took me to a recital of
the *Messiah* in Leamington, where we met Duff and some of
her holy friends. Isobel Baillie was singing the soprano role,
and, though I did not understand any of it, I was bowled over
by the beauty of the sound. I also got emotional when I heard
the fruity contralto sing, 'He was despised and rejected,' and I
remembered Clara Butt on our scratchy old gramophone on
Porgies.

I missed Bobby when he returned to Bradfield for the last
couple of weeks of term. I had already begun to hero-worship

him. I found it easy to put up with his boisterous teaching methods, because he was kind and jolly and athletic. Everyone forgave him everything.

The real challenge was yet to be faced. The youngest Winser, Susan, was my direct contemporary and so was the one on whose toes I was most likely to tread. Already a couple of drawers of the chest in the schoolroom had been cleared of her possessions to make way for my, as yet, few treasures, chief among them being my stamp collection, the greater part of which had been given to me by old Joe Babington eons ago last year in Kakamega. It was not bad, either; there were quite a lot of early British Dependencies, I remember, and an orange three-cornered from Tanou Tuva, wherever that may have been.

The schoolroom was a large airy room with two big sash windows and a popping gas fire behind a tall nursery fireguard. In the middle of the room there was a sturdy kitchen table surrounded by some equally sturdy kitchen chairs, and opposite the windows stood a tall glass-fronted cabinet with drawers beneath it. The cabinet – indeed, the whole room – was full of the signs of a girl's occupation.

Susan was the only girl in a family of three brothers. I had three sisters, so I knew a bit about girls, but my sisters were much older than me. A contemporary was a different matter, particularly one who seemed to be thought of as a delicate flower. I was ten and a half and African. Sue was eleven, a difficult age, and English. Old Annie Coleman, superannuated nannie and tyrant of the household, called her a 'scallywag', which was a bit better, but even that title was flourished like a purple heart. I was very apprehensive and was not at all sure how I was to handle the situation. It seemed to my anxious mind that Susan represented some kind of final arbiter. On her say-so depended, I thought, my continued existence at Allesley, and I was just beginning to settle down there. In fact, if it had not been so damned cold, I would be thoroughly enjoying it. But Aunt Alison said that in a couple of days she was going to drive me over to Leamington to collect Susan from New College.

But before that she took me shopping with her in Coventry. The centre of Coventry, before the *Luftwaffe* set about it four years later, was a medieval maze of narrow, noisy, crowded streets and tall echoing buildings. Cars and lorries, drays and news-vendors vied with each other to build up the decibels, and the confining pavements, muddy and wet-slippery under a leaden December sky, were crowded with people scurrying about like ants. I found it exhilarating, but incomprehensible.

'Walter, post these letters for me, will you?' said Ailie, handing me a small bundle.

'Where?'

'In the letter box over there. I'm just popping into All-woods for a moment. Wait there for me.'

I took the letters and looked around. A letter box. There was a round red thing down the road with a sort of cap on it, but it did not say anything about letters. The only possible 'box over there' was a green metal receptacle fixed to a lamp-post just across the road.

I bravely crossed when there was a gap in the traffic, and went up to this object. 'For Letters' it said. It seemed rather out of reach, but by jumping I managed to throw the letters inside. As I did so, my aunt appeared across the street. She hurried over to me.

'What on earth are you doing?' she said.

'Posting your letters.'

'Walter.' She pointed at the receptacle into which I had tossed her letters. 'What does it say?'

'For lett . . . Oh! For litter.' I felt very silly. Ailie was exasperated, but managed to laugh. 'Those were all my Mothers' Union circulars,' she said. She rescued the letters and showed me what a pillar box looked like. I must have looked crestfallen, for she took me into a cake shop and bought me a bun.

Then came the day when we went to fetch Sue. It was clearly an important event. A cake was baked and presents were bought and flowers were put in her room. The air of expectancy about the house only succeeded in lowering my spirits. Here was yet another challenge, and I was dreading it. I clambered into the back of the Morris, and we drove off. Uncle Rupert waved us off from the front door. Was he going to put down a red carpet?

It was a good drive, for Ailie was a natural teacher, and told me about Coventry and Lady Godiva, missing out the naughty bits; about Kenilworth Castle whose ruins we had to pass; and racy stories about people whose houses she pointed out to me as we went by.

'My mother was a Rotherham.' This was how she always began a family story. 'And her nephew Satz lived in that house there.' She waved her hand at yet another plain Edwardian mansion surrounded by laurels. 'He was terribly in love with me and we used to do the Lancers together in the drill hall at civic balls.' She was always good company, and today she was excited at the thought of seeing her daughter.

We finally pulled up at the gate of one more heavy turn-of-the-century building with dark laurels killing the undergrowth. There were several cars already waiting and little girls were pouring out of the big front door, pigtails waggling under severe berets, their arms loaded with pet-baskets and lacrosse sticks. Oh dear. School. Even my inexperienced eye could recognize a school when I saw one. There is a scuffed quality about school doorways which is quite unmistakeable.

Suddenly another pigtailed lacrosse-stick-bearer was staring through the car windows with eager inquisitive eyes.

'Hello, my darling. Have you got everything?'

A tooth brace was sucked into place as she nodded, without taking her eyes off me.

'Splendid. Now, do you want to come in the front with me, or in the back with Walter?'

She giggled.

'In the back – with – *him*,' she managed to whisper, and I sat as small as I could.

With another suppressed giggle she got in.

'Hello,' she said, and smiled.

'Hello,' I said.

And suddenly, unexpectedly, we were friends. I seemed to have passed the test.

We drove home to Allesley to tea in front of the fire and then, just before it became too dark to see, Sue dragged me out and down to the village to say hello to Hubert and Hilda Summers in the post office, who were our principal sweet suppliers, and to Mrs Nicks in her diminutive cottage opposite the rectory gate. (She did sewing and came in to do the ironing, Sue told me.) And to anyone else she could show me off to. Most of them I had already met, but this was different. We were a pair; and I realized with relief that my cousin was pleased to have a playmate on the premises who did not have to go home after tea. Probably more than anything else, this discovery made me feel that, possibly, Allesley could become my home.

I was so much the youngest of my family that, of all of them, only Patricia, five years my senior, was ever anything of a playmate. She was the only one who understood, I felt, my close friendship with Simiu and my feeling of kinship with him and his sister Nuffy, and all the other *totos* on the farm. As a result, Tricia and I had an understanding which sometimes was almost a conspiracy. We shared our baths and our problems. She was the only one I told about the black shoe-polish episode, and she was sympathetic in a way the others would not have been. We fought and played and explored each other's bodies. And we had elaborate games which we used to play.

Also, apart from me, she was the only one who was close to the Africans, and Nuffy was almost as close a friend to her as Simiu was to me. It was Nuffy, I suspect, who encouraged a crush Tricia developed for one of the boys who worked on the farm. Simiu disapproved of him, and I was a bit scared of him.

He was a big handsome lad with laughing eyes and a plausible smile, and Tricia who was, I suppose, about twelve and just beginning to take an interest in boys, found him very interesting indeed. One day she told me that Nuffy had arranged for her to visit him after bedtime in one of the huts that surrounded the house. She asked me to go with her because she was too frightened to go alone. This seemed the height of folly to me; the African night was not to be trifled with and, anyway, Mummy would have a fit if she found out. But she was not to be dissuaded and Nuffy, in her scornful way, had laid down a challenge. So one night, after the house was asleep, I was shaken awake and stuffed into a dressing gown, and my protests were shushed with pleas.

Fuddled with sleep and gloomy with anxiety, I was led out onto the verandah where Nuffy was waiting impatiently for us. Back in the house Father was snoring comfortably and out here on the verandah we were exposed and, in pyjamas, cruelly vulnerable to the night. Suddenly we were out in the open, and I was wide awake. The familiar compound was silent and shadowy in the moonlight, and unfriendly. A cat was yowling somewhere, and a million frogs and crickets were croaking and bubbling and whistling and seemingly from all around us, a hyena let out its eerie, mocking call:

'Cooooloooooweeeeoooo . . .' Nuffy hurried us along nervously. Tricia by this time I suspect, regretting the whole thing – and I am sure without an idea of what was expected of her – followed hesitantly. I was frankly terrified. I was in a trap: either I was about to be eaten by hyenas or, if I was lucky enough to get back, walloped by my mother's experienced hand. It was utter madness. Bed, in which I had so often lain frightened and exposed, was now the final safe haven.

As Nuffy and Tricia scuttled across the compound, I hurried after them, feeling as a soldier must feel when crossing an exposed bit of no man's land. I could feel the leopard's hot breath and I tucked in my behind as far as it would go.

We lowered our heads and scrambled into the hut which was our destination. A fire still smouldered and smoked gently in the middle, and all around the walls of the little circular hut figures were huddled under the gaudy Birmingham-made blankets that seemed to be every Kitosh's bed covering. The air was heavy with smoke and body and food smells, and Tricia and I stood there in our dressing gowns, utterly out of place and bewildered. Nuffy, thankful that her task was over, crawled under a spare blanket. If she was not instantly asleep, she gave a very good impression of being so. And nothing happened. There was no sign of Tricia's date. I should think that he had very wisely thought better of it. The risk he was taking were far greater than ours, although we did not think of this at the time.

We looked at each other. The hyena called, closer this time, I swear. The house and our beds seemed an impossible distance away. One couple woke up, and we could see two pairs of round eyes staring at us over the edge of their blanket. There was still no sign of Tricia's tryst. 'Let's go back,' she whispered, and the hyena wailed again – smack, as far as I could judge, on our route home. It was a bad moment. If we did not go back soon, we would be caught and beaten. If we did go back, we would be caught and eaten. As if to emphasize this, something could be heard snuffling about outside the hut.

'What's that?' My whisper had a squeak of terror in it.

'Probably only a porcupine. Come on.' A porcupine? With all those quills? A snake? A *leopard*? I could not move.

Nothing happened, and we began to feel silly. The couple who had been staring at us disappeared under their blanket. Finally, the fear of a certain hiding from my mother outweighed the possibility of a mauling from an unknown animal and, taking a deep breath, we sprinted back to safety. Father was still snoring. As I clambered under my mosquito net and into bed, I vowed never to leave it again. It brought Tricia to her senses, too, for she went right off her beau, much to Simiu's relief, and mine as well. In fact, a few days later she hotly denied ever fancying him. Dear Tricia – I loved her, and trusted her. We did so many things together. There was never any question that I might have refused to go with her on this abortive little adventure.

Tricia was pretty and slim and leggy; quite different from my next elder sister, Dorothy. Dolla was square and plain, with a thicket of frizzy hair, and an aloofness which none of us could penetrate. She was the individualist of the family, the puritan. She disapproved of things. This seemed very grown-up and distant. Her toys never got mixed up or shared out like the rest. What she owned she guarded jealously from the careless untidiness of the rest of us, and she tended to play by herself, with a secret life into which we felt we would not be welcomed. Her friend was Dick, the eldest and more or less adult member of the litter. We all felt that they shared knowledge and opinions which we would not understand. She tended to censure our behaviour and often corrected us firmly if our mother was not there to do it.

Dolla was often teased, which made her even more with-drawn, and yet we somehow knew that she was the keeper of the family conscience: always fiercely loyal, always honest, always straight. As children always do, we respected her and admired her solitary dignity.

Her mind was tidier than anyone else's; she was the one we turned to when we needed something, from a splint for a bird's broken wing to the name of someone we had forgotten. Even Father relied on her. 'Ask Dolla,' we were frequently told, when he did not know the answer to a question. To the day she died she was the only member of the family who answered letters promptly, and I miss her sorely as a walking research file in refreshing my memory of nearly sixty years ago. She was the most constant, and least appreciated, of us all.

Two years her senior, and different again, was Marion, the eldest sister. Though I often crept into her bed at night for warmth and companionship, I was never much more than a funny puppy to her – she was, after all, ten years older than I, and already falling desperately and sentimentally in love with anyone in her line of fire, from the local mechanic, Nigel Walsh, who had a glass eye, to Bing Crosby, whose records were the latest thing. How happy she was, I never wondered, but she often cried bitterly, either over the pieces of some gramophone record which she was trying to mend with Durofix or over a romantic novel in which she was absorbed. Sometimes she just cried. She cried easily and we took little notice, but perhaps she had a sadness which no-one, not even the parents, took the trouble to find out. My memory of her is of loud laughter or hacking sobs. Sometimes both, for she could begin by laughing and end with tears pouring down her face. As I have said before, she had hardly any schooling, but she read hungrily any cheap and easy novel she could lay her hands on. In fact, it was Marion who inspired me to teach myself to read, for she always became so passionately involved in anything she was reading that I knew that there must be something in it for me too. I taught myself to read the stories in the old copies of *Good Housekeeping*, so I cut my reader's teeth on pretty nurses and square-jawed Aston Martin drivers. The only difficulty I had was that I thought that the letter 'aitch' was pronounced 'ch', as in charming. In consequence I could not understand why the hero doffed his chat, or why the heroine was always defiantly tossing her chair.

I think Marion only had something like two term's education in total; whenever she was due to go to school, one of Father's financial crises would happen, and the school was told that Marion would not be attending this term. Her avid reading was, like mine, I suspect, self-taught.

Dorothy did a little better, she had about two years of education; and Tricia could almost be said to have been educated as she had almost four years altogether. Of course, this was still the age when it was not thought important that young ladies should be taught anything more than what would equip them to run a home and look after a man; but I doubt if that would have been more than a convenient excuse for what was little else than fecklessness on my beloved father's part.

My brother Dick, as I have said, received at least a vestige of schooling. He had the good fortune to be the proper age before the family ran seriously out of money, for he did not leave school till he was sixteen – almost a degree course by the standards of the others. He went to a rather smart school outside Nairobi called Kenton College, where the sons of most of the rich settlers went before being packed off to England to be polished. He was there long enough to show that he had talent, which, if he had only been given the chance to develop it, might have equipped him for a proper career. The headmaster tried hard to keep him there, unsuccessfully. At sixteen Dick was needed on Porgies, and his lack of drive and ambition did the rest. He was also very overweight, the result, I was told, of an early glandular deficiency, so his energy level was a joke to the family, but more than a physical burden for him.

Dick tolerated me because he was kind and gentle, in spite

of his size and uncertain temper, but I must have been a sore trial to him. His great weight made him lethargic mentally and ponderous in his movements. I must have buzzed around him like a tiresome and persistent gnat. I was a precocious and quick-witted child, and one of my enduring pleasures was to get a rise out of him, and then scream blue murder on the rare occasions when he managed to catch me. He cannot have found me anything but an entirely unnecessary excrescence on his life.

One afternoon, after the usual short but heavy rainstorm, we all went for a walk in the clear bright sunshine. About half a mile from the house, Dick decided that he no longer needed his raincoat, and tossed it to me to take home for him. I tossed it back. He got cross and so did I, but he was bigger than me and more or less a grown-up. He had all the guns. Yet I felt a great surge of injustice, and decided to stand up for my rights. The usual squabble followed, until at last the girls became bored and told me to stop making a fuss and to do what I was told.

The beauty of my decision lives with me to this day. In a flash of intuition, I knew what martyrdom must feel like. I took Dick's raincoat with enormous dignity and turned towards home. I was on the edge of a huge puddle – the sort that never dried out in the rainy season. Feeling like Edith Cavell, Sydney Carton and Joan of Arc rolled into one, I marched with firm step to the deepest part of the puddle, turned and looked back at my brother with a face of suffering. Dick was watching in disbelief. Very carefully, I laid the raincoat on the surface of the puddle. And sat on it. As the tears rolled down my cheeks (which were only just above the water) I knew, for the first time in my life, the power of an actor over his audience. It was heaven.

The martyr in me was disappointed, because eventually even Dick laughed. I was furious, but I should not have been. Years later, performing a Feydeau farce, I remembered this incident and I understood what Feydeau meant when he said that comedy is always somebody's tragedy.

VII

CHRISTMAS AT ALLESLEY WAS VERY DIFFERENT FROM anything I had known before. For one thing, it was winter and, though I had seen holly and mistletoe and Santa and his reindeer beaming benignly from every Christmas card – colonials became very homesick at Christmas – for some reason I had not reckoned on it being cold. I do not mean that I expected the weather suddenly to chirp up in the middle of December, but the fact that Christmas was of necessity an 'indoors' festival was something I had not considered. Christmas in Kenya had meant rushing out after breakfast in pyjamas, to play with one's presents.

The other, equally startling, difference was the religious one. I suppose I must have known that Christmas was the celebration of the Nativity – I had at least sung about the lowly cattle shed standing (for some reason) in Royaldavidscity, and I had surely heard about 'Mary-and-Joseph-and-the-Babe-lying-in-the-manger' – but to have this made the centrepiece of the event rather than presents and food, was surprising. Also surprising, I found, was how much I liked it that way.

Such an impression did these two things make that I can scarcely remember what Christmas on Porgies can have been like without fires and cribs and carol singing and Nativity plays and wrapping up warmly to go out. After all, the previous Christmas I had spent with my family on the edge of the Serengeti, two hundred miles from the nearest town, with a Christmas dinner of guinea fowl and tinned pears, a .22 rifle and five hundred rounds of ammunition as my principal present and the nightly cacophony of hyena and jackal, interspersed with the hollow grunt of lion.

I took to the Church side of Christmas not because I was remotely a devout little boy, but because it was so much easier to cope with than the domestic, family part. With the religious side I could be myself. And I liked the reverent hush, and the echoing organ.

Alison Winser not only took me into the circle of her family, but, to all intents and purposes, treated me as if I was a fifth child. My stocking was stuffed just as brimful as Susan's, and I was never left out of anything. Ailie herself was scrupulous in her attention and kisses; my Uncle Rupert was as absent-mindedly benign to me as he was to all his offspring; and Phil, whose job it was to be Father Christmas (though we were not supposed to know), took, I suspect, especial trouble to make me feel included.

But I found at that first Christmas at Allesley, and went on finding until I had my own wife and children around me, that receiving presents was embarrassing and awkward.

All families have traditions, and the Winser tradition was

Christmas lunch, followed by that static-ridden radio trek round the Empire, climaxed by the King's speech and standing to attention for the national anthem. Then we adjourned to the hall for presents round the tree before tea. For once the cosy stove in the hall had its doors open and gave out a bit of warmth with its acrid coke fumes. Near the stove, and reaching up the well of the stairs, was the tree, decorated with all the usual baubles and tinsel and candles. Underneath the tree, in a jumble of shapes and colours, were the presents. We all sat round on chairs, while the servants stood in a ring behind.

Phil, the major-domo, distributed the presents to squeals of delight. Each of us was allocated a special place where we displayed our presents when they had been opened, so that they could be admired before they disappeared into our lives. I always spaced mine out so that it looked as though I had more than anyone else. I dreaded Phil's words as he picked up a parcel from under the tree – 'Here's another one – for Wally.' My sense of camouflage had taught me to make the right noises and to grin expectantly as I impatiently tore off the wrapping, and to gasp with delight as the present was revealed. Even if it was something I really wanted, like a new stamp album or a Meccano racing car construction kit, I found it impossible to be unfeignedly grateful – which I am sure says more about me than about anyone else. I suppose it is one of the minor hazards of being adopted, not an important one in my case. At least I knew who and where my family was, and that they loved me and were missing me. But there is nothing to be done about not belonging. I didn't fully trust people's motives.

Apart from this minor embarrassment over the presents, Christmas at Allesley was fun and full of incident, and I found it enthralling. It still had a lingering Edwardian quality about it, with spanking afternoon walks and Boxing Day meets and port. On Christmas morning after Matins (which everyone, even the servants, was expected to attend) the family all went, armed with parcels and fruit and what Peter Sellers called 'nutritious kitchen scraps', to the Paybody Children's Home, a large black and white house standing in a hollow below the church. It was an annual ritual and, as far as I know, our only visit to the place.

We were greeted at the door by Matron in her best uniform, with the mobile children lined up behind her against the walls of the corridor. Trying to look as if this was something we did every day, we trailed behind Ailie as she made her progress, stopping like an inspecting general to have a word with a child, or do up a button, here and there. Then we moved into the wards where the bedridden children were sitting up in bed, brushed and spruce, their eyes wide with – what? – expectation? Excitement? Astonishment? We placed our offerings on the table in the middle of the ward and Matron called upon the children to give us a round of applause. The visit did not last long; after a couple of carols and a cheery wave, we retreated the way we had come, and made our way back to the rectory for lunch, our yearly duty complete.

I suppose it is silly to feel embarrassed to write this, for at the time we looked upon it as a solemn duty and our Christmas Day good work and I dare say it brightened up the children's pretty boring day, but I cannot help but find it astonishing. My own family in Africa would not have turned up its nose at any of the largesse we handed out to those little patients.

Sometimes, if he had not had too many people to speak to at the church door, my uncle, the rector, came with us in his cassock, benign and pink and gentle, and made boisterous incomprehensible jokes, and gave the children a blessing. It was better when he was there, because at least they knew who he was, since he visited them once a week. When he was not there I do not suppose the little things knew who the hell we were. I imagine it was because there was no big house in the village that we took on the mantle of the local gentry. Probably my gloriously positive aunt thought that she *was* the local gentry, and maybe she was. Certainly she had the right style.

When Christmas was over and the decorations had been taken down and the crib figures had been wrapped in tissue paper and carefully exiled till next December, it was time to think about children's parties. This, again, was a role I had to learn, and I dreaded the ordeal, for I was a shy child and did not relish the idea of meeting my own age group. And it was over these parties that Ailie taught me my first painful, but most important, social lesson. My cousin Susan was clearly a party connoisseur and checked over the invitations like an old hand, deciding in detail what she would wear to each one.

110

I must have expressed my forebodings, for Ailie dismissed them scornfully. 'You're only shy because you're thinking about yourself. You mustn't be self-centred.' And that was that. A lesson I remember whenever I have to enter a room full of strangers.

In fact, on the whole I enjoyed these parties, for they mostly consisted of food and games. I liked the food and was, I found, quite good at the games. I seldom came away from one of them without some prize or other tucked into my shoe bag next to my elastic-sided house shoes. The first time I tasted Meltis Newberry Fruits was when I won them in a game of Clumps at the home of Cinque Caldicott in Dunchurch.

However, more serious matters were looming ahead, and the day arrived when Sue and I were taken to the Bedford Stores in Leamington to buy clothes for school. Actually, it was mostly for Sue, because Christ's Hospital only expected me to provide underclothes. Just vests, in fact, but we did not realize this. So half a dozen pairs of 'Chilprufe' pants were bought for me. Then I noticed that Sue was having a whole dozen pairs bought for her. It was some time before I learnt this was not favouritism but knicker-linings. (Girls wore large bloomers that matched their dresses, and that were expected to last the week. So underneath they wore an extra pair of pants, or 'linings' which could be changed more often – twice a week?) I was packed off to have lunch with Duff while Sue and her mother bought all those items of school uniform that Christ's Hospital provided itself.

My Aunt Edith's house in York Road would indeed have

been an unsuitable place for me to live. It was dark and narrow and spinsterish, and, though I always loved going there, I was glad that I did not have to live there. The narrow stairs were steep and awkward and the only spare bedroom was tiny. The house was, if anything, colder than Allesley and the garden was not much more than a yard. Her sister Norah was already senile and subject to severe epileptic fits. What I find moving now is the thought that my beloved Duff, gentle, diffident and inexperienced, had been prepared to take me in and bring me up on the very slender resources at her disposal.

Her kitchen was the province of Mrs Townsend who lived not far away with her husband Sam. (Sam had been my grandfather's gardener.) She came every day to housekeep for Duff, as she had ever since my grandmother died. Lunch at York Road consisted delightfully of bread and dripping and a banana, and long talks to Duff and Mrs Townsend about Kenya and the family. They both remembered my family from our long-ago visit in 1926, so they were far more interested in my memories than the Winsers who had never met them. I was able to indulge myself in an orgy of reminiscence, and they prompted me to tell them about Porgies, and the family; the wild life, and the Yellow Cat; the trips to Kabrass and Simiu; and the locusts . . .

VIII

DICK WAS ALWAYS THE PESSIMIST OF THE FAMILY. THE CAR had only to run out of petrol for him to sit disconsolately on the running-board, and announce to anyone who would listen that the big end had gone. When a dark cloud hove up on the horizon, he would stare at it, suck in his breath, and breathe out heavily through his great shiny nose. 'Looks like locusts to me,' he would say.

Occasionally, of course, the pessimist strikes lucky, which confirms him in the belief that he does not shirk the truth, however harsh that truth may be.

One day a small grey-pink cloud showed up unexpectedly from the north. Everyone was quite excited because it was the dry season and rain was not expected for weeks. The cloud had what looked like wispy mares' tails trailing above it. 'Looks like locusts to me,' said Dick, and we laughed; but, as the cloud grew in size and the wispy bits began to whirr out of the sky, we stopped laughing.

These were the outriders – the scouts – looking for a likely spot of country off which the swarm could feed. With a metallic clatter of wings they settled on the nearest piece of vegetation and started to munch.

Gradually the sky grew dark till the sun was blotted out and the air became filled with the staccato beating of a myriad wings and the excited screams of predatory birds. The creatures plopped down onto flowers, maize, trees, anything that was growing, and began on supper without more ado. We realized that this swarm had settled on Porgies for its night's rest.

The migratory locust looks like a large, greyish-pink grasshopper, with those hard transparent wings, long serrated legs and the face of an indignant rabbit. Its homes are the desert lands of Arabia and the Horn of Africa, and periodically it descends like the Assyrian wolf on the fold of the fertile areas to the south in search of food. Nowadays, I gather that the locust agencies of North Africa and the Middle East have managed to control the growth of the really big swarms; but in the early nineteen-thirties very few people had any idea even of whence they came.

Porgies had experienced locust swarms before, and devastating as they were, had managed somehow to survive them. In fact, it was a great excitement when the locusts came. We children and the farm *totos* were given saucepan lids, tin cans, trumpets – anything that would make a racket – and sent out among the locusts to make as much noise as we could. The idea was to unsettle the creatures and discourage them from landing, in the hope that they would take themselves farther off – to someone else's farm, in fact – before they settled down to dinner. It did not work; indeed, I have since wondered whether locusts are stone deaf, or the first followers of heavy metal pop music. If you were lucky, they might fly on, but, if they wanted to settle, they settled.

The Africans actually welcomed the periodic locust eruptions, for dried locust provided a most welcome additional source of protein to their diet. They gathered them up and killed them, then laid them out in the sun to dry and ate them like cocktail snacks. The Japanese do something of the sort with grasshoppers, though they are better packaged. I never fancied them; they had a sort of sweaty taste which did not appeal to me. My little black friends thought I was mad. I have seen the same look of disbelief on people's faces when I tell them I don't like yoghurt.

However, this particular swarm was a monstrous one, and settled over the farm – and quite a lot of the adjoining land – like a great grey blanket. Every plant, every tree, every stalk of maize, was laden and bent over with the weight of countless locusts eating their way through the vegetation. The country-side was muffled and still, as it is in Europe after a heavy fall of snow. Birds had gorged themselves so much that some of them remained on the ground, looking bewildered, far too loaded to achieve take-off. It was impossible to walk anywhere without crunching locusts underfoot. When the car was taken out, not only did the creatures quickly smother the radiator grille and make the engine boil, but we had to put chains on the wheels because the tyre treads were immediately choked with the crushed bodies, giving them as little grip as would a road covered in ice.

We discovered this when we all piled into the car and Father drove up the road to see how widely the swarm was spread. We got as far as the boundary of Jack Gilson's farm – named, as inappropriately as ours, 'Why Worry?' – about a mile and a half away. The boundary was marked by a line of tall wattle trees, planted partly as a windbreak, but also because wattle has always been the main source of building wood in East Africa.

As we approached this belt of trees we heard the occasional crack over the noise of the engine, and wondered what the shooting was. Perhaps some fierce animal had invaded the farm, attracted by the prospect of easy pickings. Then we saw the trees.

Wattles are tall, slender trees, not unlike the English poplar, that grow to about thirty feet. They were bent so far over the road that the car could not pass and every so often a tree would give up the struggle and break in two with a loud explosion. When you think that a locust cannot weigh much more than an ounce, and that these strong, healthy trees were breaking under their combined weight, it will give some idea of the size of our swarm. Father calculated that it had blanketed an area of some twenty square miles. It was an eerie sight.

Each time a wattle cracked the disturbed locusts would whirr about for a minute or two till they found somewhere else to feed. Then they would settle down and that dead silence would envelop us again.

The next morning we waited for the swarm to take off and

wing its way to the next victims. Locusts tend to rise with the sun and move on to the next bit of succulent vegetation, gradually cutting a swathe of desert through the fertile lands.

But these did not move. It must have been a bad moment for Father, whose crops were already devastated, for the only explanation was that out of the whole stretch of central Kenya the locusts had selected our farm on which to lay their eggs, before they moved on.

In fact, the swarm stayed for about three days, suffocating everything, eating anything that grew; and their dead began to stink in the heat. Occasionally there would be a small flurry, and a few locusts would clatter about and our hopes would rise. But they soon settled again and went on nibbling.

Finally, they did take off, darkening the sky, the air full of dry rustlings, and made off in a great cloud. The land where they had been looked like a Paul Nash painting of the Flanders battlefields. Ugly stumps stuck up depressingly in a brown landscape denuded of every green thing. The farm was a desert. All the crops had been utterly consumed. In the garden not a flower was to be seen, nor a blade of grass, nor a leaf; and everywhere the reek of dead locust.

But worse was to come, for a few days later the earth began to crawl with little black creatures which began to hop along like some manic horde on the march.

The locust lays its eggs in the soil. After a few days these eggs hatch, and out come what are known as hoppers – miniature black wingless versions of their parents. The hopper grows fast and, after a few more days, it measures about a centimetre. Some lemming-like instinct seems to control it, for together with millions upon millions of other little hoppers it points its nose in a chosen direction and off it hops in search of food. It forms one unit in a monstrous carpet of little black grasshoppers, which eats as it moves. Quite soon the wings develop and in no time another massive swarm takes off, to menace anything that grows in its path.

To stop this happening on Porgies all the local farmers gathered together to try and kill off the hoppers before their wings had a chance to grow. As the huge phalanx of hoppers began to move off in a sort of formation, the first thing the farmers did was to lay a line of poisoned bran in the path of the advancing army. This, however, caused no more than a momentary hiccough. The front ranks ate the bran, died, and the ranks behind simply hopped over them and moved on. The result was unpleasant in other ways, too, for the birds and other predators who scavenged the poisoned hoppers also died, and lay about the farm, rotting and smelling to high heaven.

And the hoppers moved on.

The problem was finally solved by digging a trench in the path of the hoppers. It was about a hundred yards long and about four feet deep. The hoppers tumbled into this trench, and the ones behind tumbled in on top of them, and so on, until the trench was full. The remainder would then simply have walked over their fellows, and continued the march. But, as the trench began to fill up, so the hoppers were shovelled out and burnt on huge reeking pyres. It is a measure of the size of this potential swarm that, during the course of a week, that trench was emptied twenty-seven times.

The hoppers had been dealt with and the swarm had gone; but Porgies was virtually destroyed. I suppose Father had the farm insured – at least up to a point – but it was a crippling blow, and as a farm Porgies never again looked like prospering. Father had to look around him to see how else he could scratch a living.

It was as a direct result of the locusts that Father became, for a time, a travelling insurance agent.

Some time, in the mists of my pre-memory, Father broke his leg. The story has it that, after some serious drinking in the clubhouse attached to the golf course which they had designed and built, Father and his cronies had got into an argument, at the climax of which Father had fallen – or was he pushed? – down the front steps. He fell knee-first onto the gravel at the bottom, and one kneecap was badly fractured.

The local doctor who put him back together again made a poor job of it, and I cannot remember Father without a heavy limp. His gammy leg was always the deciding factor limiting any planned physical activity for the family. My mother became quite an expert masseuse, an activity which she practised to invariable theatrical groans and sharp intakes of breath.

He saw several doctors, both locally and in Nairobi, but to no avail. Father continued to hobble about Porgies and the pain from his knee did nothing to lengthen his temper. This did not affect us, only the unfortunate African farm boys, who stared in bewilderment as he blazed away at them in fractured Swahili laced with incoherent English. I remember one occasion when he was anxious to get some task finished by sundown and he noticed that one of the boys had absented himself without permission.

'Oi,' he shouted, to no-one in particular, 'Wapi-whatsis-name – Hyamba?'

One of the Africans diffidently explained that he had gone behind a bush to do *'geroni'*.

Father's leg must have been giving him a hard time, for without more ado he hobbled off into the bush, shouting, *'Geroni? GERONI?* I'll give him bloody *geroni.'* He disappeared, beating every bush he came to and roaring with rage.

He returned somewhat sheepishly a few minutes later, to find the offending Hyamba conscientiously fulfilling his allotted task and all the other Africans ostentatiously bent over their work to hide their broad grins. His own sense of humour got the better of him, and he threw a clod of earth at Hyamba and grinned an apology. This was followed, as he knew it would be, by general hilarity and a lot more clods of earth thrown at Hyamba. Finally, the head boy called everyone to order and peace was restored, though occasional bursts of laughter kept breaking out. Simiu and I, enchanted, watched this whole odd episode from a hiding place.

But Father never vented his temper on us children; it was left to our mother to do the walloping. The only time I can remember his displeasure being aimed at me was one day when he heard me say something crass and impertinent. He simply turned and looked at me, and my blood ran cold. There was not only boredom and irritation in that look, but a kind of fastidious detachment, as if I were a stranger. It was so unlike my mother's passionate, involved anger, which we all understood, that I have often wondered since whether his children were more of an encumbrance to him than he would ever have admitted. We were all of us so totally beneath his charming spell that even now I find myself reluctant to follow that particular path of memory. Father was our entertainer, our chum, our favourite.

After the locusts had eaten their way through the Porgies produce, funds were scarcer than ever. There was no prospect of any harvest that season; even in the tropics plant recovery does not happen overnight. So the future cannot have looked very rosy, particularly as immediate cash flow had never been the least of Father's worries. What he needed was a job that offered a quick return for his labours. To this end he became for a time a travelling insurance agent.

I do not know who put the opportunity in his way, for a less likely candidate for such a post would be hard to imagine. From the evidence of his losses hitherto, it would seem that Geoffrey Evans and insurance policies were not the most intimate of friends, and I am sure that his acquaintance with bookkeeping was not much more than a nodding one.

However, an insurance agent he became, which was lovely for me because the job involved extensive trips throughout the colony. He insisted that my mother should go with him and, as I was the only one not yet old enough to be packed off to school or wherever, it meant that I was included in these journeys. This suited me very well; I would have the undivided attention of my parents. I was excited at the prospect of travelling about, but the most enticing thought was that we would be camping out every night. What hotels there were were expensive, and Africa is full of space and sunshine. Dick was to be in charge of what was left of the farm.

Instead of a tent my mother made an enormous sort of awning which could be attached to the side of our old box-bodied Chevrolet, to form a reasonable living and sleeping space. She designed this monster herself and made it out of 'amerikani', a sort of coarse cotton material which could be bought cheaply in most of the Indian dukas (shops) around the district. She made it on her old Singer sewing machine, and I can see her almost buried behind mounds of white cotton, her nose nearly touching her chin as she worked her jaws to the rhythm of the treadle while the machine whirred up seam after endless seam.

I had a healthy respect for that machine. It had a wrought-iron guard protecting the large treadle wheel and in the centre of this guard was the Singer logo, a bobbin with crossed spindles or something. Whatever it was, it looked to me like a spider and I was fascinated by it. My mother, afraid lest I should catch my fingers in the treadle wheel, told me that if I touched it it might bite me. This I took to be some sort of challenge and I used to stalk it when it was not looking. One day, while she was sewing away, I crept up on my quarry and

My father — taken during
the First World War.

The wedding of my uncle and aunt in 1915, arranged during his brief
leave from the trenches. My mother is standing, far left, back row.
Aunt Edie is seated between and just behind the bride and groom. Aunt
Nellie, who used to take us to the pantomime, is far right in the back row
wearing her wartime Red Cross uniform. Grancy is on the bride's right.

My grandfather, seated, with my father and my brother
Dick aged about two.

My mother while we were living at Crossroads. It is virtually the only
photograph I have of her. She hated having her photograph taken.

Porgies, my earliest home.

Me, aged about eight, butterfly-hunting at Porgies.

My three sisters — from left to right,
Patricia, Marian and Dorothy — taken at Porgies.

My brother Dick.

On safari in the Serengeti, Christmas 1935.
I am in the middle with my .22 rifle, which I had just received as a
Christmas present. I was never parted from it.

On the safari — me being washed in a stream by my sisters.

Crossroads, the ugliest house we ever lived in.

Me, about to say goodbye to the family as I set
out for England, October 1936.

Me in my first Christ's
Hospital uniform.

The Winser family,
with whom I lived in England.
The rector is at the back with my
Aunt Alison. Far left, back
row, is Freddy, Philip on the
right. Front row, me, Robert
and Susan.

My three cousins. Only Robert, centre, survived the Second World War.
Freddy, on the right, was a pilot, shot down in the Middle East.
Phil, on the left, was killed at Dunkirk.

put my hand out to touch it. Something sharp jabbed into my finger and I jumped back in alarm, blood spurting from the wound.

'I told you it would bite you,' said my mother calmly, carefully replacing a darning needle into its case. I never went near that spider again.

When the tent was finished it was soaked in boiled linseed oil to make it waterproof and laid out in the sun to dry. Our neighbour, Jack Gilson, who often drove over to pass the time of day, had become very involved in the making of the tent and, when it was finally laid out, invited us all over to a party at his farm to celebrate.

As we were leaving, Dick said that the tent ought to be rolled up for the night. The rest of us thought this a boring idea, but Father agreed. 'It might rain and ruin it,' he said. In spite of our protests, Dick got out of the car and rolled the oily tent up and left it under a tree.

Jack Gilson's parties tended to be rowdy affairs, with a lot of drink flowing and guns fired off into the night in high spirits. I did not see much of these parties for I was soon put to sleep in the back of the car, covered in my mother's fur coat. I became quite accustomed to waking sharply, as a twelve-bore shotgun was let off a few feet from where I lay. We usually wove home in the early hours, Dick, the three girls and I huddled in the back as we bumped over the rough road back to Porgies.

When we reached the house on this occasion we all noticed what looked like a large glowing sausage under one of the trees.

'My tent!' my mother cried.

'Oh, yes,' said my brother pompously. 'How interesting. Spontaneous combustion.'

She could well have received a suspended sentence if she had murdered him for that remark. For that is what had happened. The heat of the sun, trapped inside the rolled-up tent, had ignited and all that was left was a tube of glowing embers. Poor Mother had to start the whole tedious process over again.

By the time the second tent was finished Tricia was back at school in Kitale and the other two girls were away working as nursemaids in various neighbourhood households. We were at last ready to pack up the car and set off on the first of our trips.

The box-bodied car, which so many people owned in Kenya in those days, was, I imagine, the forerunner of the modern Landrover. It was built like a pick-up truck, with the roof extending right to the back and supported by six slim pillars. Instead of windows there were canvas curtains which could be rolled up and fastened with ties. Let down, they were poor protection from rain, but, if it rained, you parked and waited till it stopped. On either side, above the back wheels, were two long toolboxes in place of mudguards – hence the name, box-bodied. Into this car, which was a 1930 Chevrolet with disc wheels and a square radiator grille, went all the gear we needed for a week or a fortnight, depending on how long the trip was to be: food, water, petrol, spare tyres, camp beds, and all the paraphernalia for camping in the bush.

When the car was loaded my mother's ubiquitous fur coat

was laid on the top to form a nest. This was my place. The parents sat in front and I snuggled into this nest, and had a fine view all round. It was a perfect place to travel, so long as I kept my hands and feet inside the car. I did not think much of this rule, until one hot day when I trailed a leg outside the car to get some cool breeze. We were travelling through game country with a lot of flat-topped acacia thorn trees close to the road. Suddenly a searing pain shot through my big toe and I yelled in alarm as well as distress. On examination, there was a two-inch thorn sticking right through the fleshy part of my toe. Again, it was a lesson I did not forget.

Porgies was about three thousand feet above sea level, but almost any direction we set off meant going uphill. If we went north or north-west towards Uganda, we had to skirt the slopes of Mount Elgon; if we headed east or south towards Nairobi, we ascended the plateau of Laikipia, past Eldoret and Timboroa, where the railway curved round and round upon itself to surmount the high land. From there the road plunged down to the great Rift valley and the flamingo-rimmed lakes of Nakuru and Naivasha, before passing the dead volcano of Longonot, and over the ford to Ngong where clouds of swallow-tailed butterflies rose to let the car go by. Then the long haul in bottom gear up the escarpment to the plain at the top, and Nairobi itself.

Most of the clients whom Father was hoping to enrol, or from whom he expected to collect premiums, lived either in and around Nairobi or in the Highlands: those round Mount Kenya – Nanyuki, Meru or Nyeri – or west of Nakuru –

Rongai, Lumbwa, Londiani. Wonderful names that can still bring back vividly the feel of those safaris. Of course, I had no idea where these places were – but they were names full of romance and distance and wealth and lush rolling hills. Menace, too, for Father, worrying about his schedule, muttered darkly whenever he saw a heavy rain cloud about getting stuck.

Getting stuck was the one threat that worried me whenever we travelled. Breakdowns, punctures, angry wild animals – even bandits – did not concern me unduly. But getting stuck was, for some reason, a nagging anxiety. All Kenya roads at that time were dirt roads, dusty and shiny and stretching optimistically for miles ahead in the dry weather. But in the rainy season they soon became glutinous quagmires, in which a car could quickly become embedded to its axles, the rear wheels spinning madly and messily. When this happened no amount of heaving and shoving, or stuffing branches under the tyres to give them grip was of any avail. It had been known for travellers to wait for days for help to arrive. Even wheel chains which slapped confidently against the wheel housing were often useless against the gluey mud – or came off and were lost in the morass. I became haunted by the quite groundless fear that we would get stuck and be abandoned, to perish slowly of starvation in a sea of mud. A dark cloud on the horizon can, even now, give me the prickle of a danger signal. It was silly, of course, and I knew that the reason the roads became bad was that several cars and trucks passed along them every day; but Father's sharp intake of breath as he looked morosely at a black horizon and his, 'I'm afraid the Londiani road will be impassable,' made me tremulous and more than a touch resentful, for it never seemed to occur to either of them, in that case, to abandon the effort to get through to Londiani.

In fact, I suspect that my mother enjoyed the risk, for she became buoyant when a great black storm cloud reared up ahead, and considered herself quite the expert at guiding Father round the huge water-filled rut that barred the way through to the road ahead.

Of course, we always did get through, in spite of Father's gloomy predictions, to settle down on a sunny evening on some idyllic piece of springy, game-shorn turf in the lee of tall forest trees full of monkeys and hornbills and, at night, the endless creaking of hyraxes.

Up went the tent against the side of the car, square and solid and smelling of cricket bats. Then, while my mother put a kettle on the Primus, Father and I were despatched to gather firewood, having first been warned not to walk in the long grass. We took a butterfly net with us, in case we saw any strange butterflies that Dick might find interesting, and a shotgun on the off chance of bagging a guinea fowl or francolin for the pot. When we returned, loaded with wood, a pot of tea was brewing, which we drank with condensed milk and a dash of whisky – 'to ward off the bugs,' Father insisted. We lit a fire and I got myself ready for bed while my mother cooked supper as it became dark. Then we sat round the fire while I had my supper, wrapped up in my mother's fur coat against the sudden chill of the highland evening. The busy African night soon tuned up, with frogs and crickets and hyraxes competing with jackals and hyenas and night birds. But I was used to it, and not frightened because my parents were close at hand; so I went to bed happily on my little stretcher laid across the front seat of the car on a level with the steering wheel. All I had to be careful about was not to kick the Klaxon as I turned over. Father could sleep through anything, but it made my mother nervous and she had trouble getting back to sleep. I fell asleep to the comforting murmur of their voices as they sat round the fire planning the next day's trip.

I was never allowed far from the camp on my own. This was no hardship; I have never been particularly intrepid, and my imagination could quite easily encompass the idea of some hungry animal only too eager to pounce on a tender hors d'oeuvre who had strayed too far from the nest.

Occasionally, in the more remote areas, curious tribesmen would stand at a distance, leaning on their spears, watching from another world. Their quiet seemed menacing, but they never bothered us, and would wave languidly back if I waved to them. Sometimes, if Father had an old tyre, slashed beyond repair on a rock, he would give it to them, and they accepted with alacrity. An old tyre was a great treasure, for it could be cut up and made into sandals.

In the mornings we were up with the sun, and breakfasted before it had completely dispelled the night chill or the mist that often clung to the lower-lying ground. The hornbills brayed in the trees, and the first kites and vultures began their eternal circling in search of carrion from the last night's killings. The sun began its steep tropical climb and the road ahead glinted with a million specks of mica, as we drove along, leaving a tell-tale cloud of dust behind us. For the climate was usually dry and the ground hard and unyielding, and we could make good time on our journey to the next farm or township where Father hoped to make a profitable sale.

I remember we stopped once at a prosperous set-up on the outskirts of one of the upland settlements. The house was set in sumptuous grounds at the end of a long bougainvillea-framed drive, with a rustic stone bridge across a half-dry *donga* some way down it. The farmer and his wife had one small son and a Sealyham terrier; and, while Father discussed insurance with his host and the two mothers compared notes about life, the two small boys were sent out to play together.

We did not instinctively take to each other, and there was a good deal of one-upmanship and mutual scorn bandied about. We walked up the drive with the little dog on a lead, which, for a start, seemed odd to me; our dogs on Porgies had no collars, let alone leads. But I was impressed, as I was meant to be, by the sophistication of the scene, and not a little envious of my companion's proprietorial air and his toys and his shoes and the softness of his hands. I felt very much the country hick.

When we reached the rustic bridge, the other boy stopped, picked up the terrier and put it on the parapet.

'Let's throw him in the river,' he said.

I looked over the side. It was not much of a river, more a patch of thick mud drying in the sun, with odd creatures wriggling about in it.

'He won't like it much,' I said mildly.

'Pooh – you don't know anything about dogs – it won't hurt him.' He had the lead wrapped firmly round his wrist.

'I don't think it's a very good idea . . .' I began to say, hesitantly, I admit.

What happened next was extraordinary. Grinning at me, he gave the dog a shove, and took off before my eyes. He had forgotten to let go of the lead and disappeared over the parapet.

I peered over the bridge. The little dog was struggling out onto the bank, leaving his master spreadeagled face down in the thick black mud.

I managed to pull him out onto the bank and set him on his feet. His nose, mouth and ears were full of goo and when he opened his eyes he looked just like a black-faced clown. I started to laugh, and I could not stop. He went howling down to the house to be gathered up by his mother. My mother hovered nearby, trying to help and shushing me at the same time. But I was beyond reach, consumed by an uncontrollable fit of the giggles. So I was told to go away and the two ladies disappeared into the house.

I wandered about, trying to control my giggles and was just succeeding when I passed a window. I looked in. There was my friend, stripped and showered and scarlet all over from his abrasions. His mother saw me and gave me a scowl, which set

130

me off again. I ran off round the house, doubled up with giggles. And round the corner of the house came our two fathers.

'What's going on?' I was asked.

I controlled myself and explained what had happened, sobered now under the steady gaze of my father. The boy's father frowned as I told what had happened, and I began to feel alarmed. Perhaps I should have been more sympathetic. Grown-ups can be very arbitrary when it comes to apportioning the blame.

This time my worry was unnecessary.

'Serve him right,' said the dog-owner's father. 'He's a cruel little bugger, and I hope he's learnt his lesson.' I was obscurely glad that the mother could not hear what he was saying.

The man's flash of anger bewildered me, and I looked at my father for help. He held my gaze for a moment, then gave me a solemn wink. My anxiety was eased.

I do not recall what happened after this and, as far as I can remember, the incident was not mentioned again. But I know I was grateful that we did not have tensions like that in our family.

Somewhere up in the hills Father took time off from his insurance work to consult an Indian bone-setter whose reputation was widespread. Father's knee gave him continual trouble, and he had reached the stage where anything was worth trying. Driving on those roads and in that old car was much more of a physical effort than it is today, and the frequent operation of the foot pedals was clearly a trial to him.

We camped outside the Indian's house, which was perched on the side of a hill. It was a gloomy evening, with heavy rain clouds gravid above our heads. The bone-setter greeted us solemnly. He was an imposing old man with a long grey beard and a sumptuous white turban. I suppose he must have been a Sikh. He was very hospitable and offered us cups of tea. Then my mother and I sat in the car while Father had his consultation. I imagine that the colour bar was operating even here, for we did not go into his house as guests, only as customers.

Eventually, we put up the tent before the evening rain came down, and finally Father came limping out of the house, with the dignified old gentleman beside him. He was carrying a bag and a large can. He looked pleased. We exchanged pleasantries, and the Indian retired to his house.

Father had brought a strange smell with him and when we asked what it was he held up the bag and the can.

'Oatmeal and linseed oil,' he said. 'My poultice.'

He showed us his knee, which was warm and squashy, and exuded the smell which was to become part of our lives for months afterwards.

Whether or not the new regime did him any good is hard to say. Father continued to groan and suck in his breath and grumble, and my poor mother went on being an unpaid masseuse; but, for the moment, Father was delighted, and opened a tin of oysters to celebrate. I thought they tasted of tin and was violently sick all night.

Later, after the oatmeal and linseed oil regime was left behind, Father had a leather-covered metal cage made to go round his knee as a kind of caliper, and it hung on a hook above his bed like an accusation. I do not think he was ever truly out of pain for the rest of his life.

Sometimes, to my great amazement, Father's clients actually lived in Nairobi, the seat of government and the only town of any real size in the colony. There were large shops and tall hotels and administrative buildings; hundreds of houses set in their own grounds; and the main street, Delamere Avenue, was actually a metalled road without ruts in it. My favourite place was Torr's Hotel, which was made of brick and stood like a tall wedge of red cheese at the fork of two roads. The great treat was to go to Torr's and have ice cream, which came in little bowls made of heavy metal. These bowls were marked with TORR'S HOTEL and sweated with the cold, and made a satisfactory sound as one scraped the last of the ice cream from the bottom.

When we were in Nairobi we stayed with a large burly Scottish solicitor and his wife. Their name was MacRirick, and they were childless, so I was always very spoiled there. Mrs Mac was short and round, with wispy hair and wistful eyes, and her two front teeth were crossed. Mr Mac, tall and heavy, always wore suits that hung on him as if they had been made for an even heavier man. He had a large, pale moon face, with a slow, slice-of-melon smile, and was forever scratching his behind. When I asked my mother why he did that she shushed me and whispered that he suffered from hookworm, but would not enlighten me further. I know now that it is a parasite which hooks itself into the bowel and causes severe anaemia and even more severe itching. Mr Mac was, I suppose, gradually wasting away.

They were always wanting to give me treats, and I must have been a sad disappointment, both to them and to my parents, who would surely have longed to have some time on their own, but I always burst into tears, or clung to my mother's skirts, and generally behaved in a way which I have regretted ever since. How many visits I missed to the Athi Plains to see big game, or to Torr's Hotel for ices in those heavy metal bowls, or to the Van Someren Museum to look at butterflies or birds, I shall never know. There are some things for which it is not easy to forgive oneself.

The Macs had a large town garden, surrounded by dark laurel-like hedges and at the end was a gap, rather like a lair, of smooth, well-trodden earth, over which the branches arched, making an almost waterproof canopy. Whenever I went there I met another little boy whom I called Wee Willie Winkie, after the nursery rhyme. I never learnt his real name, and I never mentioned him to my parents or to the Macs. He must have belonged next door, but I never saw him anywhere else but in the lair at the end of the garden. We often met on our visits to the Macs, and became mysterious friends. I suspect that I was as much a secret from his parents as he was from mine. We never played in either of the gardens, and our meetings had something of lovers' trysts about them, though I do not think we ever exchanged names, or even identities; we simply talked, and felt completely at ease with each other. I often wonder who he was, and what became of him, and whether he is still alive. He was the first white friend I ever had.

IX

TIME TELESCOPES ITSELF, AND WINTER HOLIDAYS AT Allesley merge into one another inextricably. There were three years before war broke out, and I find it impossible to separate them and probably it is not important. I was learning to adapt to a new environment, a new family, a new attitude; almost a new language. 'How now, thou brown cow.' My East African twang was too thin and harsh for the gentry of middle England. I learnt to keep my elbows into my sides when I cut up my meat; to write thank-you letters for presents and hospitality; I learnt that white people drove tractors and dug roads and actually served at table. Unlike Africa, wild berries in England tended to be poisonous, and all that happened if I walked through long grass was that my shoes got wet.

I also learnt not to make waves. One day my cousin Sue berated me for not grumbling and whining as the rest of the family did to their mother if they did not get their own way. That, I was told, was how all English families behaved. I knew I was being unwise but, for the sake of solidarity, I tried. Once.

Possibly my lack of conviction made me go too far, but the wintry smile I received from Ailie was not one I was prepared to risk again. I should have remembered my mother's warning about not walking in the long grass.

But Ailie, though robust, was always fair. 'You may think I'm strict,' she once said to me, 'but I shall never let you down.' When, at one point, I had to have my tonsils out, she said, as we approached the forbidding red-brick of the Coventry and Warwickshire Hospital and my heart quailed, for I had never been to hospital before, 'It is going to hurt, Walter, but you will be all right. I've never let you down, have I?'

'No,' I quavered.

'Well, and I shan't now, so you only have to be brave.'

For the first time in my life I was taught to think before I spoke. 'Now, *think*, Walter,' was more often than not her response to a question. 'There is no room in the world for mediocre people,' was one of her didactic statements. 'And you're one of them,' she sometimes added, if my behaviour had not come up to snuff. She must have known that I had much leeway to make up if I was to compete in the upper-class, public-school, conventional life into which I had been dropped. 'Sit up, Walter; don't hold your knife like a pen; always say your prayers; and stand up when a lady comes into the room.'

I am sure that she had given her youngest son Bobby the task of licking me into shape. Bobby, athletic, good-looking and my hero, would never allow me to get away with sloppiness, sometimes showing his irritation physically –

though never violently. He treated me much as an older dog will treat a puppy, with cuffs and nips – never with blows and bites. I had one useful shot in my locker: I discovered that he was fascinated by Africa, and I could always win a reprieve by telling him stories of my life and experiences, some of which I am sure I embellished shamelessly. On the whole, I think we managed a peaceful co-existence.

Bobby was Bradfield's champion javelin thrower; in fact, he would have won the Public Schools Championship by an enormous margin, if he had not overstepped the line on his final throw one spring day in 1938 at the White City. Not being strongly competitive like his brother Freddy, he took the disappointment philosophically, so the family were not made to suffer for it. He was also an avid disciple of field sports; and many a cold, raw day I spent trailing loyally around behind him, trying not to make any noise and to keep my shadow off the water while Bobby missed a weaving snipe or hauled an ugly pike out of an inhospitable winter pond. But he would suddenly give me a great hug, or blow on my hands to warm them up, and my heart would be won all over again.

Freddy, Bobby's elder brother, I held in awe. Unlike the sunny Bobby, Freddy was sombre and complex, but with a sudden smile of enormous sweetness that revealed dimples in his cheeks. He was a serious and troubled young man who sucked his thumb while reading. I tried to copy this habit, but it did not take; my thumb got all wrinkly and the roof of my mouth went into ridges. It was, I believe, understood that Freddy was destined for the Church and he was much stricter with me than the others, which seemed to me entirely fitting with his vocation. He had enormous hands and, if I irritated him, he would enclose my face in one of them. 'Face push, Wally,' he would say, and a damp thumb pressed into my neck. He was a fine tennis player and did his best to teach me the game – even in winter. I tried to please him by circling my racket behind my back in preparation for serving, but I was never much good at it. 'Oh, face push, Wally, you can do better than that. Look—' and he would execute a perfect swing, hip, toe, arm and head in poetic co-ordination. Freddy had a fastidiousness about him that set him apart from the others. Both he and his older brother Philip were destined to be killed in the war.

Phil was the eldest of the family; tall and amiable, with a round pink face like his father and a ready laugh. Even at the age of ten I recognized that Phil was no hurdle to be surmounted, as the others were. Of the four he was the most like his father, in more than looks. He was simple, trusting and unambitious, with a low intellectual threshold. Whereas both Freddy and Bobby were clearly marked out for university and leadership, Phil was happy to go to the Coventry Technical College, afterwards securing a job at the British Thompson Houston works in Rugby. In the summer he went to what used to be called the Duke of York's Camp at Southwold and was given to horseplay and sly risqué jokes. I knew he was Father Christmas because I recognized the purple sheep and cows from his printing set that were stamped all over the parcels in my stocking.

But of course it was Susan, my contemporary, who was my constant companion, friend and rival, and for whom my coming to Allesley must have needed the greatest adjustment. Luckily for me, she seemed to welcome a playmate and became more like a sister to me than my own sisters in faraway Kenya. She showed little interest in my history up to that point and, as I was a good learner, it was she, probably, who Anglicized me more than anyone.

She insisted that I learn to ride a bicycle, because she said that we would be able to go for rides together, something she had never been allowed to do on her own. This I achieved quite quickly, under the boisterous tutelage of her brother Bobby. His teaching method seemed to consist almost solely in holding me upright by the saddle at the top of the lawn and then giving me a hefty shove, so that before I had time to realize what was happening I was lying in a tangle of bicycle, laurel and nettles at the bottom. But his crude tuition soon bore fruit, and I can recall vividly the triumphant moment when I steered my way out of trouble and wobbled perilously, but still in the saddle, along the edge of the lawn. 'Now, PEDAL, Wally,' came a bawl from my cousin. 'PEDAL . . . Oh . . .' as my triumph turned to ashes and I collapsed in a heap. However, the wonderful fact that, as soon as the knack of balancing on two wheels is learnt, it is never forgotten, meant that I was soon riding confidently and even attempting some simple slalom courses set up by Bobby and contemptuously and perfectly executed by him. I gazed at his skill with hopeless admiration, and then proceeded to knock most of the sticks over, but without falling off, so I was reckoned to be moderately proficient.

Without my knowing it, this was a significant moment, because, as soon as my proficiency was reported to Ailie, I was told that we were going into Coventry to buy me a bike. In those days a child's bicycle cost about four pounds ten shillings and, as I had a little more than this in my savings bank, I was allowed to buy it for myself, which seemed to me the very peak of sophistication.

Where these savings came from I do not know. Certainly Father never sent me any money, and I do not recall doing any little jobs for which I might have been paid. I suspect that my mother scraped together whatever she could, and sent it to Duff, who probably augmented it out of her minute income. But one of the first things Ailie did for me was to open a savings account at Lloyds in Coventry, 'Because', she said, in her didactic way, 'nobody can have self-respect without money of their own.'

So into Coventry we went and a new shiny Three Spires bicycle was bought. Sue was bought a new one at the same time, which took a little of the gilt off my gingerbread, but it meant that we could ride our new bicycles home from the shop. This made me sweat with nerves, but gave me enormous subsequent confidence in negotiating traffic. Home we wobbled, along the busy Holyhead Road, with Ailie following in the Morris like a shiny black sheepdog.

With a few extra shillings I bought a silver-plated eagle to screw onto my front mudguard, so that I could call my bicycle

'Wings of the Morning', after the first British feature filmed in technicolour, which we had recently been taken to see. Sue had bought a horse for hers, she was going through the pony stage, and wanted to call her bicycle 'Trusty Steed', but this did not have quite the poetic resonance of 'Wings of the Morning'. So, after some heavy hints, which I refused to recognize, that a gentleman would give things up for a lady and in the film 'Wings of the Morning' had been a horse anyway, she compromised and called her trusty steed 'Wings of the Evening', but it did not trip so easily off the tongue as mine, much to her chagrin, and to my own secret delight.

Our bicycles were much loved, much polished and much used and, on subsequent holidays, we went on many rides around the district, venturing further and further afield as our confidence grew. We were armed with packets of sandwiches, water bottles and puncture outfits, and a few pennies for Snofruits from the Stop-me-and-Buy-one man, and felt very intrepid.

Sue also introduced me to my first taste of the heady joys of acting. She had learnt 'Up the airy mountain, down the rushy glen' and 'There was a little grasshopper for ever on the jump' at New College, and was longing for an excuse to recite them to her family. So we decided to call ourselves 'The Antics' and imposed the tyranny of our performances, not only on the family and staff at the rectory, but also on the local branches of the Mothers' Union, the WI and any other organization we could coerce into a submissive hour.

At first my role was confined to singing jolly sea shanties

like 'The Mermaid', and making offstage noises to illustrate Susan's recitation; but I soon discovered the drawbacks of the latter when my Uncle Rupert ordered me to be quiet as he could not hear the poems. I was not sorry to lose the sound-effects job; not only was the artistic scope very limited, but Sue got all the kudos. So we began to write our plays with titles like *The Red Magician*, and we performed in the school-room with gusto and lightning costume and character changes. Our greatest success was when we were asked to give a repeat performance of one of our masterpieces before an invited audience from the village, to raise money for the church spire. I suspect that we enjoyed ourselves far more than our audiences, but it was many years later that I under-stood my rudimentary actor's instinct which made me uneasy with my stage partner's inability to forget herself when she was acting. She thought nothing of stopping the performance to explain a point, or she would giggle helplessly at the thought of herself in some outlandish costume. Not only did I not understand, but I felt in my bones that it was wrong. I know now, of course, that stage giggles, reprehensible as they are (for they show a lack of concentration) are never self-directed; they are always about some external incongruity: the banality of the line one is expected to say, or the fact that the dignified lady playing opposite is quite unconscious of the clothes-peg dangling from her wig. Sue's giggles were the self-conscious laughter of the amateur afraid of making a fool of herself.

The Winsers were not a theatre-going family. In fact,

almost the only time I went near a theatre was the annual visit to the pantomime at Coventry's brand-new Hippodrome; and my first experience of a traditional English pantomime that Christmas of my arrival in England was entrancing. I do not remember which one it was, but that is part of the charm – pantomimes are always the same, so that you meet an old friend at every change of scene. That first time, at the front of the circle, with an ice cream, and a box of chocolates whizzing up and down the row, was a revelation. I had no idea what a pantomime was, and did not understand why my blood stirred at the sight of the curtain lit expectantly by the footlights, while the orchestra played a medley of popular songs. But the moment the curtain went up, I was pulled into the wonderland of light and colour and magic. The sound of a line of tap-shoes hitting the stage in well-drilled precision as the chorus of gorgeous, long-legged, smiling girls went into the opening number is a thrill I shall never forget. It goes without saying that I fell deeply in love with the principal boy, usually someone like Vera Lennox or Pat Kirkwood, and usually I picked out one member of the chorus and followed her adoringly through all her changes, from 'Member of the Royal Hunt' to the final stunning ballroom scene, when she swirled down to the front with her partner in the closing walk-down.

Then there were the speciality acts, especially the funny ones. The Cairoli Brothers, a group of clowns who turned garden hoses into trumpets and chair legs into xylophones – always about to fail, but ending in triumph. And my all-time favourites – Wilson, Kepple and Betty. This act consisted of two stringy old men with droopy moustaches, dressed in tarbooshes and white nighties, who did a deadpan dance on a small sand tray to the tune of 'The Sheikh of Araby'. Sandwiched between them was Betty, a luscious busty girl in baggy trousers and a sequinned bra. Wilson, Kepple and Betty danced very slowly and solemnly back and forth on their sand tray, with appropriate arm and neck movements, like an absurd Egyptian frieze. I heard many years later that the Betty used to change each season, because, not only did Wilson and Kepple guard her jealously from consorting with other members of the company, but their expectations of her tended to be above and beyond the strict call of her contract. Stories of the current Betty escaping from the locked bedroom of her digs by tying the bed sheets together and absailing to freedom may have been apocryphal, but were very persistent at the time. Be that as it may, they were, for me, one of the funniest music hall acts I ever saw; and I first experienced them in pantomime in Coventry.

That first visit to the theatre in the winter of 1936–7 was, it turned out, the regular Christmas present to all her nephews and nieces – real and pretend – of a serious and severe old lady with pince-nez and a silky moustache, called Aunt Nellie Rotherham. She lived alone in a large Victorian house called Rosehill in Coundon, on the outskirts of Coventry. She was uncommonly plain, with tiny watchful eyes and the voice of a breathy tenor, and everyone adored her.

The Rotherhams were one of the big Coventry families. Originally they were watchmakers of considerable renown and the family influence eventually spread to the law as well as commerce; Rotherham and Sons are still one of the city's most respected legal firms, with a measured ponderousness in their dealings commensurate with their dignity. So Aunt Nellie was thought of as well-off. To me she was fabulous; I had never seen anything like her, or her house, before. Rosehill was dark and comfortable with too much furniture covered in brown plush, brocade curtains and sober velour tablecloths with tassels. Like many spinsters, she identified with children and I responded to her straightaway, and we remained fond friends till her death in the Sixties.

Her pantomime parties began when we were deposited at the Hippodrome in time for the matinée (parents were banned till after tea). Aunt Nellie took the entire front row of the Dress Circle (or so it seemed to me) and sat among us like an inscrutable Chinese emperor, her pince-nez and moustache glistening between a black felt hat and a fur tippet. Her very presence, severe yet benign, was quite enough to make us all behave.

After the show we were taken in a fleet of cars to Rosehill for a sumptuous tea. The big dining-room table was laden with crackers, jellies, sandwiches, biscuits and cakes of every description. I did not know whether to believe it or not.

The pièce de résistance came when tea was over. Aunt Nellie had accumulated throughout her life a large collection of Victorian and Edwardian toys and just once a year, at her pantomime party, they were brought out and we were allowed to play with them. We were enjoined to treat them with respect, but I am sure that this warning was never necessary as they inspired respect. Those toys were of a craftsmanship and ingenuity and robustness that have never since been matched, and I hope that they are now in a museum somewhere. There was a hurdy-gurdy, all to scale, that not only played a tune when wound up, but the organ-grinder turned his handle and his monkey did a little dance; birdcages with incredibly lifelike birds that sang; dancing animals, and steam engines, and dolls of every description and race. To someone whose experience hitherto had been two dilapidated Dinky toys and an old pedal car, one wheel of which was made from the top of a brace and bit, Aunt Nellie's toys were pure *Arabian Nights*. It would be some years before I experienced Hamley's at Christmas, but the effect was similar.

I do not suppose that Aunt Nellie Rotherham was as rich as we thought her, for she ended her days in a rather sad and stuffy private hotel called The Hylands where her own jar of marmalade and bottle of Worcestershire Sauce marked her permanent place in the dining room; but to me she was the wealthiest of benefactors, and her brusque offhand manner the communication of royalty. I could just claim a family connection. 'My mother was a Rotherham,' – Ailie's invariable preamble to any family saga – meant that Nellie was some sort of cousin. As I knew that Ailie was Father's cousin, I was proud to claim her as a relative.

There were other contacts whom Ailie was keen for me to make, mostly old people who remembered my father – 'Oh, 'e 'ad such a twinkle in 'is eye, 'ad your dad,' – or who had some family connection with my great-great aunt, Marian Evans, the novelist George Eliot. I was taken to Arbury Hall, the home of the Fitzroy Newdegates whose estate my great grand-father Isaac had managed; and to Nuneaton, where until very recently there was even a George Eliot billiard hall. I am sure that it was a kindly and thoughtful effort to make me feel that I belonged, and I grew accustomed to feeling that I was on display, and to listening to long and rambling reminiscences of life at the turn of the century. I only wish that I could remember them.

But one place I do recall, because I must have paid several visits; this was to a village outside Nuneaton called Chilvers Coton, where the Misses Robinson lived, in Coton House. They were three spinsters, Kitty, Nellie and a third whose name I forget, so let us call her Hettie. Kitty, the youngest, best-looking and by far the most on-the-spot, had, on her own proud and (I always thought) rather sly admission, been a girlfriend of my father's in their youth. As a result of this, I was given a great welcome at Coton House and was often left there for tea, while Aunt Ailie went about her Mothers' Union business in the area (she was the diocesan president). The tea was brought in by Mary Keeling, the maid who was clearly the lynchpin of the household and got the three old ladies organized with napkins and tables and footstools, while Kitty regaled me with stories of balls and parties and dinners that she had been to with Father. Nellie, meanwhile, pink and stout and distraite, would ask me every three or four minutes whether I took sugar in my tea, and supervised the endless conveyor belt of bread and butter and cake onto my plate. I think Nellie was as daft as a brush, but no-one remarked upon her eccentric behaviour, so maybe I am wrong, though I was constantly aware of her benign but off-key presence and the simplest conversation with her was an adventure into uncharted seas.

Hettie, meanwhile, was quite silent and sat in a corner, knitting ceaselessly, and having silent but animated conversations with herself. Hettie's knitting was the source of a long-running embarrassment for me. At my very first visit, she announced that she would knit me a pullover for Christmas. Kitty was patient.

'Not this Christmas, dear. It's only two weeks away.'

Hettie was crestfallen. 'Well, a birthday, then,' she suggested. Kitty sniffed. 'When is your birthday, Walter?' I told her, May. 'Hmph,' said Kitty. 'Well, perhaps . . .'

In fact, it was the following Christmas before the pullover was ready. It was a famous present by then; there had been a lot of talk about it, so the whole family was intrigued when I unwrapped it.

I thought it looked a bit small.

'It will soon stretch,' I was told. 'Put it on.' It was as I was doing so that I discovered that the neck was just about wide enough to take a small orange and, however much I pulled, only a small tuft of hair would show through.

The pullover was enquired after whenever I went to Coton House and every sort of excuse was aired: that it was at the cleaners, because we were afraid that it might shrink; that I had just spilt soup down it; simply that for once I had forgotten to put it on. Actually, it had long since been relegated to Mrs Nicks' basket of cleaning rags; but, as far as the dear Misses Robinson knew, I wore it almost every day.

I soon realized that to the old people who knew him Father was the handsome, debonair life and soul of every party. I wonder now if they would have recognized the somewhat weather-beaten figure trying desperately to make ends meet in an occupation for which he was temperamentally unsuited.

X

FATHER'S FARMING METHODS WERE NEVER WHAT YOU might call planned; he was too much a creature of whim. So some new crop or method of cultivation was usually tried out before the last had had an opportunity to prove itself. Forethought was not one of his guiding principles, so he tended to catch himself unprepared for the results of what he did. A good example of this was grass-burning. The long rank savannah grass each year became entangled and dried up, and was a considerable fire hazard. So, before it was burned off, several things, like wind direction, weather, and what lay in the path of the burn, needed to be taken into consideration. This was not Father's way. He would stop the car and gaze with narrowed eyes at a large stretch of brown and tangled grass.

'That looks as if it would go,' he'd say, lighting a cigarette. 'Yes . . . Let's see.' And he would toss the lighted match into a mat of tinder.

The result was invariably panic in one direction or another. If it was not some unfortunate labourer's *boma* that had to be saved, then it was some stock that had got trapped in the path of the blaze. One day it was Porgies itself that was threatened. All the boys had to be called away from whatever they were doing, given gunny sacks and told to beat the flames out as they approached at a steady pace before the evening breeze. It was touch and go for a time, as patches of ash left for dead fanned themselves back into life, and the fire crept nearer and nearer. It was not until 'Milwaukee', the wooden privy at the edge of the vegetable patch, went up like a torch and the can of Kerrol fluid exploded as the fire reached the cultivated part of the garden, that it finally subsided to wisps of smoke, leaving the house isolated in acres of grey acrid wasteland, and all the furniture covered in a fine layer of ash. My mother must have finally read the riot act to him, for I do not remember Father setting the grass on fire again with quite so much abandon after that.

I loved it, though, because the burning grass put up all manner of creatures, and the bee-eaters had a field day, gorging on all the bugs fleeing for their lives before the crackle and heat that was chasing them and whistling like a football crowd at the end of a match. Duiker and bushbuck, jackals and serval cats, as well as a host of smaller animals, careered out of the path of the holocaust, their fear of man quite overshadowed by their terror of fire. The garden was often host to several trembling creatures, standing together when normally they would be either chasing, or running away from, each other. My mother, though, disliked the whole thing. Not only did she resent having her home threatened in

152

this cavalier fashion, but she said the house would be used by snakes as a shelter, and with several children running about without shoes, it was not on. I can see her point.

I suppose it must finally have become obvious to Father that Porgies would never be able to support us under his makeshift husbandry and the threat of natural disasters. Then came the locusts, and his short-lived career as an insurance salesman. Even to such an inveterate optimist, the end could not have seemed far off.

But he had one final shot in his locker. He decided, on fairly slender evidence, that somewhere on the farm was a rich vein of gold. All we had to do was find it. With his rather hazy memories of the Australian Gold Rush to back him up, he was sure it would be easy, and our fortunes would be made. It is another illustration of my mother's patient support that she never opposed Father's scheme.

I should explain that at about this time – the early Thirties – gold had been discovered in workable quantities in various parts of the colony, and productive mines had been opened up not very far from the farm, in an area stretching from the township of Kakamega to Kisumu on the shores of Lake Victoria. It was known as No. 2 Area, for some reason.

We had known for some time that there were gold deposits about the farm. Occasionally a lump of quartz with which the place was liberally scattered would reveal the tell-tale thin gleaming thread, and Father's ears would prick up. But nothing was ever done about it, until some Norwegian prospectors, a family called Sundi, appeared in the neighbourhood, and found in Father an eager disciple. With all the paraphernalia of the prospector – divining rods, gold rings hanging from a piece of thread, little hammers in their belts and dollies and pans in their luggage – they soon had him and Dick, who was not his father's son for nothing, convinced that they were sitting on a fortune.

As if to prove this, they discovered that almost any handful of dirt from the bed of a stream (Dick insisted on calling it an 'alluvial deposit'), or any piece of crushed quartz, when panned out in water, showed two or three enticing yellow specks in the bottom of the pan after everything else had been washed away. Quartz is the chief gold-bearing ore and, as I mentioned before, the farm was rich in these white outcrops. Even I felt the excitement of breaking open a lump of quartz and seeing the shining golden thread running through it. For Father it must have been intoxicating: El Dorado was right there under his feet. Normal human greed did the rest. And the Sundis' eyes glittered at him in encouragement.

Father started in quite a small way between insurance trips. He broke off chunks of quartz from the more likely looking outcrops, crushed them by hand in large dollies – which were like tall iron pestle and mortars; and then panned them down by hand. This he had learnt from the old Australian pros- pectors. The pan was rather like a frying pan without a handle, but with a lip scooped out on one side. Into this pan you dumped a manageable amount of dirt, or crushed quartz, or river bed, and, by carefully washing away all the lighter material, pushing it out of the lip of the pan with your

154

thumb, you were left in the end with a small deposit of clean sand. Any gold present in the stuff you were panning would surely be in this final deposit because, being heavier than the rest of the dirt, it would be left in the bottom of the pan till last. By the time you reached this stage, it was easy to see any grains of gold nestling among the clean washed sand.

We all became quite adept at this, for it was easy to do and really very exciting. There was always the hope of finding a real nugget – a hope, I may add, which was never fulfilled.

By taking carefully labelled samples of soil and rock it was easy to discover which way the reef ran. At least, that was Father's theory. The trouble was that, as far as we could see, there was gold everywhere on the farm. Wherever we took a sample some gold usually showed up – never very much, but always some. It was, therefore, very difficult to decide just where the fabulous reef was to be found. So, in order not to be caught empty-handed when quartering the farm for likely places, Father took to carrying a small hammer about with him, tucked into his belt like a six-gun. With this hammer he could give a whack to any piece of rock he came across, so as to split it open and persuade it to deliver up its gleaming secret.

Clearly this strain of gold-prospector's fever was a virulent one, because several of the neighbouring farmers began to take a similar interest in their land – though rather furtively, so as not to let their more sensible wives into the secret. One in particular, our nearest neighbour, Jack Gilson who lived up the road at 'Why Worry?', was badly infected. In fact, I suspect that, if it had not been for his wife, Queenie, a tough, pike-faced virago from Johannesburg, with her hard-hearted and hard-headed good sense, Jack might well have succumbed to Father's enthusiasm, with equally disastrous results.

Even so, Jack, too, for a time carried around a little hammer in his belt. I can remember, as he and Father stood around talking, one of them would casually pick up a lump of rock and, with an expert tap with his hammer, split it neatly in half. I could never do it; it required a sense of rhythm which I hadn't learnt.

One morning Jack drove over to Porgies to see how the prospecting was getting on, and he was invited in for a cup of tea. He was a gentle, rather bumbling man, with an expression on his face as though he was just about to be struck by a brilliant idea. We were all very fond of him, and felt sorry that he had to live with Queenie. He had two children, Graham and Ann, whom we despised, because their clothes were always immaculate and we thought them snooty. Actually, I do not imagine that they were all that keen on us; we were a pretty scruffy collection.

At any rate, on this particular morning Jack stood smiling hopefully in our living room, while my mother poured him his cup of tea.

'My, that's a fine teapot,' he exclaimed, pointing, not at the enamel pot that my mother was holding but at a pretty Victorian lustre pot standing in pride of place on the mantel-shelf.

'Yes,' she said, 'it's all I have left of a teaset which belonged to my grandmother.'

'Very nice indeed,' said Jack, and picked it up to admire it. Without thinking, he took the little hammer from his belt and gave the teapot a sharp tap, neatly smashing it into four pieces. Everybody froze. Jack was calmly examining the broken pieces for signs of gold, his expression as hopeful as ever. Mother never felt quite the same about him again.

The first serious efforts to find the magic seam of gold marked a turning point in the life of the farm, for the Africans were taken off their usual jobs and set to dig pits at various strategic sites decided on by the swing of a gold ring (my mother's wedding ring) or the nosedive of a divining rod. It was at that moment – though probably not even he realized it – that Father finally admitted that he was no farmer. In retrospect, it has an elegiac feel to it, for farming was what brought the family to Africa. But certainly from then on Father made no attempt to farm the land. I can only suppose that his insurance work kept the wolf from the door, though even I, at seven or so, was aware that it was never very far off. Indeed, it was not long before Mother was trying to sell our bananas and was sewing endless ore-sample bags for the big mines, to try and make ends meet. But that was yet a few months ahead.

Quite soon the area round the house within a radius of about a mile was honeycombed with holes like the ones in which Piglet found the Heffalump, ten or fifteen feet deep. Dangerous, too; tiger-traps, their mouths and spoil soon bearded over by the fast-growing tropical grass. The contents of these pits were taken down to the nearest stream, which we called the Little Porgies, to be washed through for signs of the elusive gold.

Once or twice an ox fell down one of these pits and had to be winched out, bellowing tragically. Tricia and I liked to explore them, mostly for the frisson of fear, for the pits soon became dank and dripping and smelt of moles, with huge resentful-looking toads crouching at the bottom. Often snakes, too, coiled up and resting from the heat of the day. Sometimes bats and small animals colonized them, so we never knew what we might find.

One of these pits was more elaborate than the others. It was deeper and long, like the grave for a giant. It also had crude steps cut into one side, and a sort of gallery halfway down, wide enough to stand on comfortably. Probably it had shown more promise of gold than the other pits. One day Nuffy and I climbed down onto this shelf. It seemed an excellent place on which to keep her long-standing determination to show me how to *do it*.

When she heard from her brother Simiu of my lamentable lack of sexual experience, she was most disturbed, and decided that it was clearly her job to take me in hand. I was always eager to learn and had gathered from Simiu that it was not an unpleasant experience, so I gladly fell in with her plan, and followed her willingly along the beaten path that led past the large pit.

Down we climbed, into the musty, rodent-smelling gloom; not to the bottom, of course. That was dark and wet and probably full of snakes. But to the nice dry shelf halfway down. There was just enough room for our purpose, if we stood up. Not an ideal position, perhaps, but at seven I was not to know this. Nuffy, at all events, seemed to think it quite adequate.

She told me what to do, and I co-operated as best I could with my extremely insufficient equipment. However, having managed with some difficulty to manoeuvre into a critical and potential position, I heard somebody laughing.

Nuffy and I looked up in disbelief. My sister Tricia, hands on hips, was standing on the rim of the pit looking down at us. If she had laughed any more heartily she might have lost her balance and joined the snakes at the bottom, and, at that moment, I would have been delighted if she had. Anger or outrage at what we were trying to do I could have understood; derision seemed unfair. However, it served its purpose, I suppose, for once again I had failed by an inch (I may be flattering myself here) to know the ultimate experience. Nuffy was livid; she, at least, knew what she was missing.

But none of these pits produced gold of measurable quantity, and they were soon abandoned to the snakes and the voles and the heffalumps. Father had more ambitious plans.

The Sundis descended on the farm from their Valhalla on Mount Elgon, and persuaded Father and Dick that their best and easiest chance of wresting gold from Porgies was to exploit the famous alluvial deposits – in other words, to scrape the beds of the streams which bounded our property on three sides. I imagine that Father must have entered into some sort of partnership with them, for they more or less moved in – at any rate, they seemed for a time always to be there. They had names like Haakon and Odin. (Odin was typically tall and blond and my sisters swooned over him.) They were large and friendly and fit, and talked endlessly in their odd sing-song English. There was one woman whom we all called Girlie – all bust and muscle and long gold hair in a plait – who, I am sure, was a wife and mother – they all seemed the same ageless age to me, each one scrubbed and bland and smiling.

One of them, though, was different. He was dark and squat and frog-like, with one wandering eye. He was supposed to be a wizard with the pan, and used to sit endlessly by the stream side, humming tunelessly as he panned out his sample. We never knew his name, but he came to be called 'Who', because my mother was once caught singing the popular song:

'Who stole my heart away?
Who makes me dream all day?'

while he sat patiently waiting in his long johns as she darned a hole in the seat of his trousers. He, like the others, was friendly and garrulous, but we children must have been a sore trial to him, for his eye made us giggle uncontrollably. My mother got cross with us, but that only made matters worse.

At first the alluvial work consisted of scooping up buck-etsful of stuff from the bed of a stream, and panning them out by the side of the prettiest pools. There was one particularly enchanting spot, which had clearly been an ancient crossing-place, where the water glided over smooth flat rocks and the banks sloped gently down on either side. Just a little way upstream was a deepish pool, with a large tree-branch stretching out low over the water, where I could sit and catch catfish with a bent pin on a length of string. Nearby was a wild fig tree where the bright green pigeons and parakeets came in flocks to gorge in the branches and the butterflies came down to drink from the mudbanks. There were never enough hours in the day to do and see all there was around me. Hiamba, our former tractor driver, became very adept with the pan, and he would be content to crouch all day on the bank, gently washing away the dross, and always becoming excited at the few grains he would end up with. Once one of the Sundis teased him by dropping a gold nugget one of them had found years before into Hiamba's pan. His euphoria when he saw it gleaming in his pan was so great that it was difficult to explain the trick played on him.

Eventually it was decided that the amount of gold in two of the streams justified a rather more elaborate scheme of extraction.

The stream that bordered one side of the farm was called Cheptoygen and, before it joined the larger Kamakoya, it did a wide meander in a distant corner of the farm. Part of this corner was the large wood where Father had planted coffee in the early days. This had reverted to a bit of jungle and tangled scrub, which grew luxuriously where the two streams joined and flowed secretly through it, dark and dangerous. The far bank of the Kamakoya marked the boundary of the native reserve, where we were not allowed to go without permission, though I sometimes went there with my black friends, feeling very bold and privileged.

Father and his advisers decided to divert the Cheptoygen by digging a trench across the neck of the meander, leaving a half-mile loop of disused river bed, which could be scooped up and washed out for the gold it might contain.

Of course, this was a major operation and the entire labour force of the farm was diverted, to dig the trench and shift the soil, build a dam, and construct the special flume along the side of the trench, for cleaning the soil which was supposed to contain our fortune. The Africans were glad of the work, for there was none to be had on the farm; that had been abandoned long since. What Father paid them with I have no idea, but they all seemed to work cheerfully enough. So I must assume he paid them somehow.

It was a very exciting time for me. The stretch of water that was being cut off had flowed between high banks, with the lush tropical growth leaning extravagantly down on either side. The banks were full of holes, in which lived every species of vole and rat and snake and other creepy-crawlies. The pools were full of fish – mostly tilapia, and big black catfish with long whiskers. The butterflies were more varied here, because, as well as the ordinary whites and yellows of the savannah, there were lustrous floppy ones of the forest and riverside – beautiful papilios – the technical name for the shimmering blue and green Swallowtails; mother-of-pearl butterflies the size of a small saucer, with delicate black tails; the multi-coloured gleaming ones that settled on the flowers and the mud; and, of course, the big strong aristocratic bullies – the charaxes – that circled the high trees and swooped down occasionally to drive their more delicate brethren from some choice piece of dung or rotting fruit. Great dragonflies and beetles were there, and sometimes bees and wasps and hornets, to which I gave a wide berth. A hornet had once got up the sleeve of my vest, and had stung me several times, reducing me to panic before someone had removed my vest so that it could go on its way. It was a terrifying experience, and I have treated hornets with the greatest respect ever since.

The trees round the workings were full of birds of every hue – and cry – and there were monkeys swaying in the treetops as they foraged for fruit. Ancient tortoises could sometimes be seen, wending their ponderous way through the centuries; iguanas, too, occasionally clattered nervously away, their dry hides sounding metallic as they brushed against the undergrowth. Once or twice a porcupine, carefully avoided by man and dog because of its quills, scuttered off into the trees, and from time to time one heard, rather than saw, a bushbuck or waterbuck, woken suddenly from its siesta, crashing through the bush out of the dangerous scent of man.

So there was always something new going on, and Simiu and I would get down to the workings as early as we could, so as to miss nothing. Or else we would join Father and the others as they made their slow way down in the car.

Father's gammy leg made it very difficult to walk the couple of miles down to the river workings, but his financial straits were such that he could not, finally, even afford the petrol for the car. The car, however, was, I suppose, some sort of status symbol, for, instead of using the old farm wagon, he had four of the draughtoxen hitched up to the old Chevrolet. With one of the *totos* to lead them, they trundled slowly off past the old maize fields and the overgrown coffee plantation, with Father solemnly steering and Dick lolling beside him, occasionally yelling at one of the oxen. I loved it, because I could jump off and chase after a butterfly or anything I happened to see, and catch up and jump aboard again without any difficulty.

Once the work on the diversion trench was finished, the great day came when the river was finally dammed with rocks and tree trunks and a last few sandbags. As the water rose behind the dam, the last few spadefuls were dug out that separated the river bank from the new trench. The water quickly found the easiest route, so that the last reinforcements could be slopped onto the dam. Very soon the ancient course of the river was reduced to a trickle. The level fell away as the water drained downhill; and within a day the old curve of the stream was reduced to a series of standing pools, full of fish and other creatures, and the ancient bed of the stream was exposed, primeval and dank and dangerous. It was wonderful.

Upstream of the dam and parallel to the new trench was the flume, which could be opened or shut by means of a sliding gate. This was to be lined with zinc and mercury and used to wash the dirt as it was scooped out of the exposed bed of the dammed-up stream. Zinc and mercury combined act as a magnet to gold, so that if there was any gold washing down with all the rest of the stuff from the stream, it would stick to this coating. At the end of the day the mercury would be scraped off the zinc lining, and then squeezed through chamois leather. It was a sight that always delighted me – the pure clean drops of mercury forcing their way through the chamois like silver tears, leaving any gold lying clean and dry on the inside of the leather. Poor Father. The resulting little mound of gold was always pathetically meagre.

Once the dam was finished, the stream soon settled into its new route, cutting its own way under the banks and washing out the bed clear to the stones at the bottom. With tropical vegetation soon covering over the scars, the old stream bed quickly took on the rather sinister look of some ancient swamp, the water getting lower and dirtier and more stagnant every day. As the pools dried out, the stranded fish became more and more frantic, stirring up the mud as they swam round in ever-decreasing circles. They could sometimes be scooped out with a shovel onto the bank, and very peculiar some of them were, flopping about on the grass. I suppose now that some may have been quite rare primitive breeds, but none of us had any interest in fish, other than as something to eat, and very unappetizing some of them looked.

One morning, as one of the Africans was straddling a small pool, one leg on the bank and the other on an islet, there was a sudden warning shout. We all looked up, and the entire workings became silent. The man in the stream was frozen in a crouched position, his eyes wide with terror. Very leisurely, a huge snake eased its head out of a hole in the bank. It had a large blue and white ring-marking round its neck. Immediately below the straddled legs of the petrified African it paused and looked around suspiciously. Nobody moved. Scarcely anyone breathed. After an eternity, it slowly moved on and finally nosed its way into another hole further down the bank. We all watched it, fascinated, as its muscles expanded and contracted in its progress back into the earth. When its tail finally slipped out of the first hole and slid into the other one, all hell broke loose and the poor African fainted. Dick reckoned it must have been about twelve feet long. We never saw it again, but everyone gave that stretch of bank a wide berth thereafter.

It cannot be said that the efforts to find gold on Porgies ever looked like succeeding. There probably was – probably still is – a rich seam somewhere in that area. I've since been told it could have been something to do with the water table. But Father simply did not have the resources to do a proper survey and, like most of his other enterprises, it slowly fizzled out. It must have been with some despair that, after fifteen years, my parents finally decided that enough was enough and that Porgies must be left to its fate. There was no money left with which to pay the Africans, so the river workings had to be abandoned. The maize fields, already neglected, were matted and overgrown; the coffee bushes swamped by undergrowth beneath the trees where Father had planted them; the citrus plantation was entangled by wild fig and attendant creepers, with the undernourished fruit rotting on the ground; and even my mother's faithful banana plantation was beginning to be choked by weeds and looted by the local Africans. The house itself, never exactly classical in its lines, was sagging a bit, and the corrugated iron roof-sheets were starting to work loose. With no funds to keep it in check, tropical vegetation wastes no time in reclaiming its own.

It was at this low point in our fortunes that my parents made up their minds that it was time I went to school. I cannot imagine where they got the money from to do it, for Tricia was already there. I suspect that both our fees were paid by a neighbouring farmer we all called W. J.

W. J. Carter was a Francophile bachelor who farmed a neat and prosperous stretch on the far side of the stream we called Little Porgies. We all thought him a bit of a joke, for he was always neatly dressed in dark clothes and sported a stick and an immaculate pith helmet. He was portly and pompous; he had a neat Hercule Poirot moustache; and I am sure that I once saw him in spats. We were wrong about him, though; he was immensely generous and, I suspect, lonely; and he bore a great admiration and affection for my mother. It is more than likely that he saw what a tough row she had to hoe keeping the family going. Father never liked him and made a great many jokes at his expense and became cross because he said W. J. always smelt of garlic. Perhaps he felt threatened. Certainly, my mother usually took his side and defended him gently whenever we jeered. I know that it was he who paid my passage when I came to England. We never knew what W. J. stood for.

The W. J. Carter scenario is the most likely, for, having

decided to pack up and leave Porgies, I would have been an encumbrance to my parents while they looked for work and a place to live. Much more convenient to have me safely at school. Besides, I was eight, so it was time I began to climb the educational ladder. I was dreading it. I had never left home before; I had not taken to the other white children I had so far met, and I would have to wear shoes. I had no idea what to expect, but that was enough to be going on with.

So in January 1935, grey with grief and terror, but at least with my sister Tricia holding my hand, I was deposited at Kitale European School, in the care of the headmaster, Mr Barton, a cadaverous gloomy man with dark sad eyes and a disappointed mouth.

Homesickness is a tunnel of despair and loneliness from which there seems to be no escape, and to which there is no apparent end. I did not rationalize homesickness until many years later, when, due to the demands of work, Evangeline and I were separated only months after being married. We were very hard up, and I could not see any possible end to our long separation. I had forgotten what homesickness felt like, and how incapacitating it is. I suppose it is a form of bereavement and like bereavement it is the inability to see an end to it that makes it so overpowering. You grow out of it eventually, but not before it has had its pound of flesh.

Be that as it may, it was homesickness that overshadowed and spoiled my five terms at Kitale. There was a long avenue of flamboyant trees that led from the main road to the front of the school; I would look on this avenue as the road to prison,

168

or the road to freedom, depending upon which way I was facing. In the same way, we sang a hymn to an identical tune at the beginning and end of every term: 'Lord, behold us with thy blessing,' at the beginning of term, and 'Lord, dismiss us with thy blessing,' at the end. The words 'behold' and 'dismiss' came to represent enslavement and release. Being left under Mr Barton's disillusioned gaze on that first day did nothing to reassure me.

Mr Barton was, I have every reason to believe, a perfectly ordinary, reasonably harmless man. But I had never been left in the charge of a stranger before and to see the dilapidated old Chev putter off down the avenue with my parents inside, and to realize that I was at the mercy of this grey remote man, made me uneasy. It was an unease that remained with me until Mr Barton left the school a couple of terms later. Tricia was not much of a comfort; she, too, looked pretty scared. I did not understand until later that that was her habitual expression when confronted by authority.

I seem to remember that we stood around in silence until Mr Barton sent us off to collect our things, and make ourselves known to Miss Roberts, the matron.

Kitale School was a handsome, white, red-roofed colonial-government style of building of two storeys. There was a long cool colonnaded verandah running the whole length of the building on both floors. I seldom ventured upstairs, because that was where the seniors had their classrooms, and I left before I had a chance to become a senior.

In front of this main building was a circular driveway, at the end of the avenue, with a round bed of canna lilies and a flagpole, all very neat and formal and Public Works Department style. Tricia and I used to walk round and round this flower bed, and down to the end of the avenue and back, during break, which was about the only time we had to spend together. As I remember it, I was usually crying and Tricia comforting me. Only once was it the other way round when, about a fortnight into my first term, she suddenly spotted the old Porgies sofa on the back of a lorry, with Africans sitting on it, going past the end of the avenue – presumably on its way to the sale rooms. I did not realize the significance of this, but Tricia gave a loud wail, and the image has stayed with me ever since, as a sort of symbol of the ending of our Porgies idyll.

To the side of the main building was another, also white and cool and tidy, with red rooftiles. This contained the dormitories, ablutions, kitchens and dining hall, and was the domain of the aforementioned matron, Miss Roberts. Clarissa. She was a large, Junoesque person who looked like an angry Wyandotte hen. She was a prying bully and was the first human being of whom I was mortally afraid. Philip Abrahams, the headboy, ran her a close second – but more of him anon. Clarissa Roberts succeeded in making me cry every other day, for every other day we were given clotted cream instead of butter and jam for tea. I had never been good about cream, particularly the clotty sort; it made me feel sick and I heaved at every mouthful. Clarissa would not let me get down till I had eaten it all. It was not like ordinary clotted cream – more like the skim off the top of boiled milk; so it was runny, and covered the whole plate, and made the bread soggy. Clarissa who, on a subsequent visit to England, told Aunt Edie what a sweet, cheerful little boy I was, would stand over me as I heaved and wept in the by now deserted dining hall, exercising what I suppose she thought was improving discipline.

My other ogre was Philip Abrahams. He cannot have been more than thirteen or so, but to me he was a grown-up. Tall and blond, with a permanent frown on his handsome brow, he was in charge of 'no talking' in the dorm. His favourite trick was to creep up behind a chattering junior – usually me, for even then I was garrulous – and deliver a stinging blow to the side of the head. Bedtime was often accompanied by a ringing skull and a warm ear, for I never learnt to be more circumspect. Philip had a younger brother, with red hair and freckles, who was as gentle as his brother was harsh.

But Miss Tatham I adored. She had a spanking new Ford V8 tourer, with shiny wire wheels and a dicky. She drove up to the school every morning with a spritely crunch of tyres on the gravel, and strode smartly into the commonroom with a cheerful wave. She wore long dark skirts and high-necked white blouses – invariably, it now seems to me – rather tight over the bosom. And very modern rimless spectacles. I suppose she was a true spinster, but I thought her very glamorous. This was probably because she encouraged me, and was kind. To get an EXCELLENT stamp in my exercise book from her was the high point of any day. The stamp had a sort of Stakhanovite picture of a steel works – all red and steaming and *achieving*. Of course, I fell in love with her.

Apart from the scourge of homesickness, I do not think that I was particularly unhappy at Kitale; I simply never understood why I had to be there. I liked the work, and was good at it, because I had started later than the others; I was older and therefore quicker to learn. I was gregarious and made friends easily. I was fairly good at games (though terrified of the hard hockey ball). And, because of Dick, I knew quite a lot about butterflies, which gave me a certain cachet. But my regular bouts of homesickness were a real scourge. What made it worse was that other children did not seem to be affected by it, so it was always something of which I was vaguely ashamed. The only other person – apart from Tricia, but she was a girl so different – who seemed obviously to suffer from it was a Dutch farm boy called Nels. The British Boers were rough and guttural and we were supposed to despise them. But I liked Nels because he was homesick too. He was big and raw-boned with almost white hair, *en brosse*, and almost illiterate, but lonely and miserable, and my heart went out to him. We used to sit in the classroom writing home, while everyone else was shouting and playing outside, and we fed each other's suffering. I remember outlining the mark of a tear which had plopped onto the paper, and labelling it, 'Sob, sob.'

That first term came to an end at last. We sang 'Lord dismiss us,' at assembly, and a motley collection of luggage was piled up on the front verandah, to be loaded onto cars, trucks, lorries, even a horse and cart, as parents arrived to collect their offspring. The Dutch boy, Nels, was mercilessly teased that his father would turn up with a wagon and a full span of oxen; actually he came in a neat, rather modern saloon car with about four handsome brothers, who gathered up Nels with great whoops of joy, and bore him off in triumph. Our near neighbour, Captain Buswell, picked up Richard and Agnes and Pauline in a tall, dignified Model T Ford whose very high clearance was much favoured on the muddy and rutted Kenya roads. Mr Barton stood around smiling remotely, to see off his charges, while Tricia and I waited anxiously as more and more children were carted off. We knew we were not going back to Porgies, and, as the waiting numbers dwindled, we began to wonder whether actually our parents had got the day wrong and would not turn up at all; or that they had lost their way; or, worst of all, as far as I was concerned, they had got stuck. But finally, and not quite the last, the battered old Chev clattered up the avenue and we ran to meet it – the chariot that was to bear us to heaven, even though we did not know where heaven was going to be this holiday.

Joe and Kath Babington lived in a pleasant homestead on a wooded ridge some way up the slopes of Mount Elgon. Father had had to take a job as underground manager in one of the gold mines near Kakamega, a fairly rough and raucous township on the edge of the goldfields, and our parents decided that Joe's place was more suitable for Tricia and me to spend that first post-Porgies holiday than the rather raffish boarding-house in which they had landed up. If I had had any choice in the matter, I would probably have agreed with them, but Tricia would have begged to differ.

Joe Babington was a tall, elderly New Zealander; we knew this because he always wore a smart Kiwi hat – like the stiff tall hat worn by Baden Powell in all those pictures of him which used to hang in Scout halls, only darker. Joe was slim and upright and he had a pink flanelette face with a long nose that – I swear – twitched. He also had pale blue, hot little eyes that followed the girls about, a fact which even I noticed, though I could not imagine why; they were just my sisters and not worth watching. I liked him though. He was interested in things like stamps and animals and was a keen butterfly collector. (I suspect that this was why we were at Joe's – Dick was a frequent visitor and they would spend hours together discussing food plants or the wing-pattern variants of some insignificant little insect.) And it was quite different country from what I was used to at Porgies. Below the house ran a stream, bounding down the mountainside in falls and pools, with thick, lush forest almost hiding it. But this forest was different from Kabrass which we visited from Porgies on butterfly expeditions; here were mostly succulents and huge ferns, usually dripping with moisture. The rocks were covered with bright green moss, and creepers hung in rope-like swags from the taller trees. As a result, of course, the animal and insect and bird life were different, too. These forest butterflies were large and floppy and slow, with shining upper parts and dead-leaf camouflage on the underside of their wings. When the graceful mother-of-pearl butterfly glided past, like a great leaf fallen from one of the trees, you caught the occasional gleam of opal, as it made its stately progress from one noisome bit of food to another. These forests round Joe's home I found fascinating and just a bit scary. Tricia disliked them, though whether this was because of their eeriness or because Joe always insisted on helping her over obstacles with his attentive hands, I never discovered. She was always loyal to our parents' decisions, and did not confide her misgivings about Joe till many years later.

That holiday passed in a haze of impressions, but always there was the dread of going back to school. And, of course, before long I was again in the echoing assembly hall, sodden with tears, with 'Lord, behold us with thy blessing,' ringing cheerfully and threateningly round my head, and Tricia, already a segregated stranger, standing tall and pretty among the girls on the other side of the hall.

XI

EVEN THAT FIRST TIME, GOING AWAY TO SCHOOL FROM Allesley did not produce the crippling bouts of home-sickness that leaving home in Kenya had inflicted on me. I was scared, all right, but this was different. It was not my true home that I was leaving and, though I sympathised with Sue as she wiped her tears away with her pigtails and did my best to be forlorn, this was a huge adventure that was opening up before me: a wide-eyed challenge which had been trundling towards me for almost a year. Anyway, you can only be torn away from one mother, and I had done that. Somehow, separation in England seemed puny compared to the distances of Kenya. The bustling security of the Southern Railway was a far cry from the tenuous, unreliable dirt roads which, in Kenya, were my only link with home – roads which, as Father liked gloomily to say, were often impassable. I was hardened to separation.

It fell to Duff, as usual, to take me through London, to catch the Housey Special at Victoria. I think she found these journeys painful; it seemed so often to be her lot to push me off into the unknown; but, of course, to me it was really another voyage of exploration. We caught the train from Coventry to Euston, a dark and looming place which seemed to know that most journeys from it ended in the Black Country. But we soon left the cavernous gloom of Euston and plunged down into the underground, which is one aspect of life that has changed little during my lifetime. I have always enjoyed the tube: the swaying trains thrusting busily at you from the tunnel; the heavy sigh and bump of the sliding doors; and the anxious throb of the electric motor, dying in a rallentando before the train moves off again.

As I remember it, we arrived at Victoria Station with ample time to spare, due to both of us being sufferers from train fever; so Duff took me to the news theatre, perched up some steps off the booking hall. There were news theatres, I think, at all the mainline stations in London, delightful time-wasters for those who arrived at their station with a half-hour to spare. They were miniature cinemas showing news, current affairs and cartoon films (called Silly Symphonies) as well as comedies and travelogues. 'And so we say farewell to Hong Kong, Pearl of the East.' And Joe McDokes leering round from behind an enormous bowling wood. I loved the news theatres and when I was old enough to cross London alone I always tried to get to Victoria with time enough to get one-and-sixpence worth of noisy, hollow-sounding escapism, before the school special left.

The new boys and their parents had a coach reserved for them, so that they were not thrown into the noisy, boisterous

177

scrum of the old hands, showing off their holiday acquisitions, or playing some elaborately prepared practical joke. Besides, we did not yet have our uniforms and would be bewildered and out of place among the hordes of long blue coats and yellow stockings which had swamped Victoria Station in the twenty minutes before the special left. Perhaps this was for the benefit of our guardians, who would have been no match for the noise and general lawlessness. We settled diffidently, parents and boys alike, into our compartment, and stared wide-eyed at each other across the space between us.

At the station – Christ's Hospital has its own station, one stop south of Horsham – there was a great deal of skylarking and dashing about before the monitors had managed to fall everyone in by houses and march them off to their various destinations. As far as I remember, we new boys, plus our parental appendages, were put into a bus and driven off to our prep houses, leaving the station platform piled high with trunks, sent 'Passenger's Luggage in Advance'; eight hundred and fifty of them, which the school carter was gradually working his way through.

When we arrived we were separated into those destined for Prep A and those for Prep B. Mr Willink was waiting for us on the steps of Prep B, looking like a benevolent Neville Chamberlain, and welcomed us with his fluting tenor voice and his bobbing Adam's apple. On the train journey we had made the acquaintance of another new boy called, I think, Short, and his parents, who were a tall solemn clergyman with tinted glasses and his rather forbidding wife, and we clung to

178

each other like lone survivors from a shipwreck, though it was obvious we had nothing in common. But, in the whole alarming process of initiation – being issued with a uniform and a house number, having a locker allocated in the day-room, and a bed and settle in the dormitory – it was some comfort to have a familiar scared face to smile at occasionally. I suspect that Duff and Short's scary parents felt the same, for they were still together when we finally bade them a rather shaky farewell; I believe that Duff used to send them Christmas cards.

Each new boy was allocated a minder, called a 'nursemaid' – a marginally more experienced little boy – to lead him through the runways and passages to classrooms, dormitories, dining hall, playing fields, and to pilot him round the hazardous shoals and reefs of custom and tradition, which were the unchangeable liturgy of English boarding-school life. Christ's Hospital is a large school with four hundred years of tradition to feed on, and the first thing a new boy – a new master, too, I suspect – had to do was to learn the language and the unwritten laws. Perhaps only the Church is as tied to ritual and tradition as the English public school, and, though both are at last making efforts to break the mould, in 1937 it was still all taken extremely seriously by both boys and staff. Those few daring rebels (of whom I was emphatically not one) who tried to take the system on had a pretty thin time of it.

My nursemaid was a little terrier called Allen. (I never knew his first name; not until we were great beings called

Grecians was it acceptable to call each other by our Christian names.) He was about half my size, with a deep bass voice and a permanently damp and sore-looking upper lip. He made up in hector what he lacked in cubits, and for those first weeks I felt like a clumsy calf with a sheepdog nipping at my heels. I was mortally afraid of him, which I am sure was his intention. Once I was released from his angry but kindly care, we scarcely ever crossed paths again. On moving to the Upper School we were put in different houses and into different streams and, anyway, we were never well cast as what Americans call 'asshole buddies'. But, if he is still around to read this, I should like to recall my debt of gratitude. In his alarming way he defended me fiercely against the uncharitable and intolerant world of small boys en masse, and he gave me such a thorough schooling that first cold, frightening term that I was soon able to do my usual camouflage act of not making waves, and became, if not an ideal schoolboy, at least a reasonably popular and successful one.

In those first weeks bed was the one place where I could feel safe. Safe to be myself, and think my thoughts and have a cry, or a comforting cuddle of my private parts. I cannot claim that I was ever homesick at Housey. I was by this time something of a connoisseur of homesickness; the loss of my mother and my home were, as it were, one remove away, a distant and fading pain, never to be replaced by missing my adoptive home, kind and loving though it was. If I was lonely, it was the hugeness of the world into which I had been plunged; if I cried, it was having to cope with so much by myself. But homesickness it was not. Homesickness is desolation, and I was not desolate at Housey.

Nevertheless, Christ's Hospital I found a huge and daunting place, with few comforts and little time to stand and stare. I was always cold, except in bed. I was learning the argot; learning to learn; learning to compete with children who for the first time in my life were cleverer than I was. And then there was the climate; after Kenya it was harsh and dark and wet and freezing. I developed an intimate and ongoing relationship with the chilblain. The only warm places, apart from bed, I could find were within a few inches of the dayroom radiators, and we pressed our fingers and bottoms and heels up against them whenever we could find a space. No-one thought to tell us that that was the way to get chilblains. Perhaps I am unjust – perhaps dear Mr Willink warbled at us, with a dance of his Adam's apple, about fresh air and exercise, but we took no heed. Warmth was what we were after, too pressing a need to allow for other considerations.

So my bed was the resting place from challenge. I was allowed my own rug to supplement the basic ration of blankets. This was a treat, because we had few things of our own. Everything we wore, except vests and pyjamas, was provided by the school; any other comforts of a personal nature, like woolly scarves or teddy bears, were definitely discouraged. Bedtime, then, with my rug and pyjamas, was a kind of haven in those first terms. I was certainly challenged at Housey; but I was not homesick.

And, compared with my experiences at Kitale, it was safe and civilized. I never felt physically threatened as I had at Kitale, and, though even at Housey human rights were things that only much older boys could expect, there was a rough kind of justice and fairness that I felt I could trust. There were no despots; in fact, I think only once in my seven years at Christ's Hospital did I come across any serious bullying, and that was soon dealt with. Of course, it was bliss at the end of term to sleep in a soft bed after the mattress-on-boards in those long bleak dormitories; or to get up into clothes that felt weightless, instead of the long heavy blue coat and coarse knee-breeches; or to tuck into good home-cooked food off a pretty plate. Yet I never felt the incredible flood of release as I had when we sang 'Lord, dismiss us with thy blessing,' and saw the trunks piled high on the long verandah and listened for the first chuggings of parental cars trundling up the flamboyant avenue to take us back to freedom.

Not merely freedom, but adventure too, were in those first holidays from Kitale. As Father moved from job to job, so we moved from house to house. Each one had new smells, new people, new places to explore. After Joe Babington's place, the second home Tricia and I came back to was amazing. It must have marked the nadir of Father's fortunes, and how Mummy coped with it passes all understanding. To us it was paradise.

Father had passed on to the job of manager of a trio of exhausted Bedford lorries, which seemed to be a branch of an outfit called Goldfields Transport. This organization served the new gold fields round Kakamega; and, if the lorries were exhausted, the state of the house was terminal.

'House' we called it, but it hardly deserved the name. It was actually not much more than a shack. It had cane walls and a flat corrugated-iron roof, and cane blinds that rolled down over the gaping empty windows. It was divided roughly into four or five 'rooms'. (Cane walls again. No doors at all.) And the whole had been simply thrown up on a piece of level ground beside a crossroads – the only feature of a featureless bit of land about ten miles from Asembo Bay on Lake Victoria. The garden consisted of one flat-topped acacia thorn tree, under which the lorries parked like a group of animals sheltering from the sun. As far as I can remember there was not another building in sight. With great originality, the house was called 'Crossroads'.

The floors, which I suppose were once of beaten earth, were by now of trampled dust, at least an inch deep. It must have been a nightmare to keep even a vestige of cleanliness. I loved it.

The tatty old Bedfords were used mainly for collecting stores from the railhead at Kisumu for the several gold mines round Kakamega, and one of the African drivers, a laughing friendly young man, used to let me travel with him in the cab, and sometimes he would let me steer when there was nothing else in sight on the road. When, on a subsequent holiday (and from yet another 'home') the local policeman, nicknamed (obscurely to me) 'Phyllis' Wright, found out that I had the rudiments of driving at my fingertips, so to speak, he took me in hand and allowed me actually to drive his big Ford V8. I could not reach the pedals with my feet, so I only drove on the flat bits where it was not necessary to change gear. He could reach the pedals with his long legs from the passenger seat. I thoroughly enjoyed this, and I can only guess in retrospect that Phyllis got a kick out of it too. He used to let me search for stamps among the waste paper behind the Kisumu police station. Nobody seemed to think his behaviour was odd, so I can only assume that it was not. It was certainly entirely innocent.

It was at Crossroads that I developed measles, and was kept in a darkened room for a fortnight and allowed to choose what I ate. My diet was thus an invariable one of guinea-fowl sandwiches and Del Monte tinned pears. Dick shot the guinea fowl down by the Yala River, and I suppose the pears came from the Indian *duka* in Asembo.

My mother never grumbled, though it must have been a nightmare house, with a permanent carpet of dust and, of course, no running water. We put large lumps of alum in the water tanks to settle the muck and kill the bugs. (Tricia and I used to dare each other to lick the alum; it was disgusting and dried up your spit.) And, naturally, all water had to be boiled. It must also have been an anxious time for Mummy; Father's jobs did not seem ever to last very long, and Dick at that time was the only one who was earning his keep. But she was endlessly cheerful, singing about the place in her reedy voice. As a result, we were all very happy at Crossroads. The girls were all of an age to fall in love, and there were plenty of young men about to play with; and I had my air rifle and the lorries and freedom to do more or less as I liked. Dorothy and I used to go for walks in the short evenings, when she was mooning over a chap with a bandage on his leg, called Archie something, and she taught me the words of 'Red Sails in the Sunset' with tears in her eyes. It all seemed a bit funny to me, but Dorothy was not always the most friendly of my sisters, so it was a kind of bonus.

The only drawback of Crossroads was that the dust floors were a breeding ground for the jigger which, as I have said, likes to lay its eggs in a sac under the toenails, with unpleasant results if not dealt with straightaway. So every evening meant a session with needle and iodine, as Mummy dug the wretched things out.

But all too soon the spectre of school loomed on the horizon, till came the morning when, grey with tears and foreboding, Tricia and I were loaded (literally) onto the Goldfield Transport bus to Kitale. This was really a pantechnicon with expanded wire sides, wooden benches and a flat roof on which the luggage was piled – along with chickens, goats, vegetables, furniture and several Africans. It was a journey of some sixty miles, and we clung to each other, the only whites in a cheerfully chattering, singing and odorous crowd of marketgoers, as we watched our mother's dumpy, hopeless little figure, clutching a damp handkerchief (for she cried as much as we did) slowly disappear as we rounded the first corner.

'Lord, behold us . . .', the smell, and the impersonal indifference of school closed around us again. Mr Barton's sad, pallid face, and brassy Clarissa Roberts and her skimmed cream for tea; harsh games in which I had to fit into a team; stinging cuffs from Philip Abrahams, and the ridicule of those who did not seem to know what homesickness meant. Unwillingly, but with growing familiarity, I grew the tough skin of institutional life and settled into the ways, and the friends, where I could rub along without bumping into too many sharp edges.

And always there was the balm of Miss Tatham with her mild myopic eyes, pretty smile and motherly bosom to remind me that gentleness still existed, and inspire me to get that EXCELLENT stamp in my exercise book. And occasionally Tricia and I could escape for a few minutes during break and walk up and down the avenue, holding hands and talking about home.

The Avenue. It was the main artery of Christ's Hospital and ran the whole length of the school. We marched up it to meals and chapel, walked up it to classes, and ran up and down it on runs. It was broken in the centre by the great quad in front of big school, the chapel and the enormous dining hall. Here the entire eight hundred and fifty boys ate their meals at sixteen long tables, one to each house. The two prep tables were down at one end under a platform by a large window, where the ancient and terrifying school monitors had their breakfast in solemn grandeur, waited on by boys

186

from the prep houses, whom they treated with lordly condescension. One morning I was taken right back to Kitale when one of these noble beasts – he was called Lawrence and he was Senior Grecian – leapt down and gave me a cuff for talking during grace. But the cuff had none of Philip Abraham's malice; it was a firm magisterial rebuke from God. Not the same thing at all.

The dining hall was the domain of Noel Sargent, the hall warden, a bull-like Frenchman with a small moustache and neat footwork. His station was a dais halfway down the hall, under an enormous painting by Antonio Verrio, recording the granting of the Royal Charter to the school.

'Sammy' Sargent's dominance was never in doubt; to be reprimanded by Sam, or worse still, reported to one's housemaster, was an unthinkable horror; it was with some surprise, a few years later when I was playing rugby for the school colts of which he had charge, that I discovered a warm and funny human being. Later still, when I was in his senior French class, he treated me with unexpected leniency after I had cribbed a translation of the Apostles' Creed from a French prayer book. It was probably my naivety in not expecting to be rumbled by a native-born Frenchman that must have amused him, for he was not as angry as I expected him to be. Another trait that helped to make him a 'character' was that he always kept his classroom windows open on cold days to keep the air fresh, and tight closed on hot summer days to keep the room cool. He said that that was what they did in France; we were learning French: QED.

But meals at Housey, under Sam's austere gaze, were squalid affairs for a small boy in the late thirties. Not only did he have to do all the serving, but the tradition of 'passing down' meant that he always had the scraggiest helpings of unpopular dishes, and the smallest of popular ones. Not only that, when the seniors had finished their helpings (often before the junior had sat down) they passed down their dirty plates too. The result was that the smallest boys had to bolt their unprepossessing food behind a rampart of dirty plates – which it was then their duty or 'trade' to clear away as well. It was one tradition I was able to break when I became senior enough. I was surprised no-one had done so before, but table manners were not high on the agenda at that time.

Apart from meals, the two prep houses were segregated from the rest of the school, except for the occasional special chapel service. On these occasions we sat in the gallery at the east end of the chapel, on a level with the huge and ugly Frank Brangwyn murals that ran the length of the building. These depicted a selection of scenes with a religious signifi-cance, like the *Miraculous Draft of Fishes*, or (if I am not mistaken) *St Columba Landing on Iona*. I remember feeling sorry for all those makers of our religious history: they all seemed to be suffering from severe attacks of arthritis – all their bones and joints appeared to be painfully swollen. And every man Jack of them as ugly as sin. They quite distracted me from the theme of the service. And scared me a bit, too.

The chapel was long and narrow, with all the pews facing each other down both sides; from the gallery, we could look down the whole length of the building. One of my abiding memories is of the headmaster, the alarming H. L. O. Flecker, always the last to go up to receive communion, walking back the length of the chapel in his rather greasy academic hood, shiny head bent, and an expression of public gravity on his face. I always wondered what solemn message he had received that had not been vouchsafed to the rest of us. In those early days 'Oily' Flecker was a terrifying Olympian figure, and even in the prep, tales of his amazing rages were legendary. I had so little to do with him during my time at Housey that I can neither confirm nor deny these stories, for he taught classics, and I was a modern linguist.

The two prep houses sat cosily at the east end of the avenue; the Upper School was like those spaces on ancient maps which say 'here be dragons': full of strange and scary creatures and customs, and to which we were to be thrown in a couple of terms' time. Pat Maltby – just 'Maltby' of course within the confines of the school – had a mother who was a friend of Ailie's, and we occasionally saw each other in the holidays. He sometimes walked down the avenue from his house (Thornton A) to visit me after Sunday morning chapel. He was a gentle, short-sighted, dreamy fellow, who surprised me by his kindness to a much younger boy whom he did not know very well. Hierarchy had an iron grip, and I was experienced enough to know that any real friendship between us would be frowned upon; we could never, outside these Sunday meetings, do much more than acknowledge each other's presence. Nevertheless, I determined that his house was the one I would ask for when the time came for me to 'go up'. I discovered, when I did graduate to Thornton A, that Pat was a fine long-distance runner – a solitary, dreamer's hobby, entirely consistent with the way I saw him; he could never concentrate for long enough to make headway in a team; his sense of humour always let him down at moments of serious crisis. He told me about life in the Upper with an amused detachment, picking absently at his upper lip with a finger-nail, his voice jerking up and down the scale as it began its uncertain journey to manhood. Pat was eventually taken away from Housey and sent, I think, to Wellington. He had a strange obsession with climbing roofs, a hazardous occupation which landed him in constant trouble, for he always got caught. I think he must have had some kind of breakdown before he left, but if he did, it was so low-key that none of us knew anything about it. None of us knew much about him, come to that. He was the cat that walked by itself; but, though he never had to protect me physically, I regarded him as my protector for as long as I needed one. I don't think he enjoyed Housey much.

The end of term was an altogether more boisterous business than I had known at Kitale. The Housey Special left Christ's Hospital Station for Victoria at an unearthly hour – I know it was still dark in the winter terms – so the last breakfast (of hard-boiled eggs and tea) had about it the feel of Christmas morning – hurried and excited and expectant. Odd bits and pieces of luggage lay to hand waiting to be trailed to the station as soon as breakfast was over. Our trunks had, of

190

course, already gone 'Passenger's Luggage in Advance', and such was the efficiency of the railways then that they were often waiting for us on the doorstep when we got home.

I seem to think that the hard-boiled eggs were replaced by something less dangerous later on, after several railwaymen and inhabitants of mid-Surrey had been struck at level crossings and signal boxes as the Housey Special rattled through, and complaints were made to the relevant quarters. The journey to London was always rowdy, but a kind of discipline was maintained by the unfortunate members of staff assigned to travel with the boys, and very seldom was any damage done. It was, however, fortunate for the travelling public that the train was a special, reserved entirely for the school; the green, lightweight-seeming, seaside-resort-heading trains of the old Southern Railway seemed a touch frail for all that mayhem.

I was not yet trusted to see myself across London and it was invariably Duff, pink-nosed and myopic, puffing away at a Gold Flake, who was waiting for me at the barrier; who bought me a meal at the ABC just outside Victoria, before catching the tube to Euston and the bicycles and machine tools and the sturdy, serious London Midland and Scottish trains in their maroon livery, destined for the grim dark towns of the Black Country. Sometimes, though, we went to Leamington first instead of Coventry, and that meant leisurely Paddington, and the chocolate-and-cream country trains of the Great Western Railway that stopped at places like Kingham and Banbury, before bread and dripping with

Mrs Townsend in the kitchen at York Road, waiting for Ailie to pick me up and drive me back to Allesley. To the safe certainties of a Midlands, middle-class country rectory, with none of the rackety excitement of the life in the sun and the dust and the insecurity . . .

Another holiday. Another home. Christmas 1935. This time it was 'Kiefie's', an African type *boma* of a few rondavels on a piece of beaten earth, with one or two trees and a neat patch of garden. It was quite close to Crossroads, and simple enough in accommodation, but it must have been another world to my mother. It was clean, and the rolled mud-and-dung floors allowed only ordinary dust to accumulate. There were trees and green grass, birds and butterflies; and, unlike Crossroads, it had been looked after with love and attention. It belonged to Keith Brand who was small and dapper and reminded me of the advert for Sharp's toffees. But he was kind; he had moved out to stay with a friend so that we could have somewhere more salubrious to live, and because he knew we were homeless. After Crossroads it was Buckingham Palace. Our old friend, Frank Kirk, who eventually married Marion after falling serially for the other two girls, lived in a pleasant house on a hill with a distant view of the lake only a few miles away from us. I think the family felt less abandoned at Kiefie's.

I had been told that Joe Babington was giving me his stamp collection, so when my mother said there was a big surprise, I was quite severely put out to discover that no, the surprise was that we were going on safari to the Serengeti for Christmas. I soon got over my disappointment when I saw all the gear waiting to be loaded into the cars – tents and guns and butterfly nets and Father's ancient binoculars and great boxes of food; as well as Joe's stamps.

Frank was to come with us in his old Chev, even more decrepit than ours, but between them they could carry us all; and one early morning the week before Christmas we trundled off while there was only a glimmer of light to the east, and headed towards Tanganyika, a couple of days' journey to the south. After Kericho the land became more and more empty and we chugged on over the dirt roads – some of them little more than tracks. In spite of Dick's gloomy prognostications about broken springs or 'big ends' going, it was a great adventure. Dick was not coming with us, so he could enjoy being a Cassandra.

After two days we crossed a dry sandy river bed below the Loita hills, entered what Frank said must be Tanganyika and set up our main camp among a grove of flat-topped trees. The land fell away to a thickly wooded stream on one side and rose to a rocky knoll, the home of a large family of dog-faced baboons, on the other. Father studied the map and announced that we were two hundred miles from the nearest human habitation. This I rather doubt now, but at the time I was deeply impressed. I felt that we had left the world far behind.

Almost the first thing Father did after we had pitched camp was to shoot a zebra which had strayed to within a quarter of a mile of us. He hoped that it would attract a lion, but all it did was to make the night raucous with the insane laughter of hyenas and the yapping and growling of jackal. We often heard the hollow rumbling of a lion not far away, but it did not come near the kill. However, it was enough to make me wonder how the family could go on sleeping through all that racket. In fact, it sounded very close indeed, and sometimes the baboons thought so too, for they would suddenly start up an hysterical barking, probably, Father told me in the morning, because there had been a leopard about. Leopards are very partial to baboon, apparently. Lion or leopard, I was grateful that whatever it was was after them and not me.

It was a lovely camp. We still had the balloon-like awning that Mummy had made for our insurance trips from Porgies. There were a couple of tents for Frank and the girls, and an enormous tarpaulin strung from trees for shade. I slept in my usual place on a stretcher across the front seat of the car. With so many people around me, I was only a little scared of the night sounds, but I tucked my knees up to my chin when I heard the lion; I was not going to tempt him with my toes sticking out into the night.

On Christmas morning Frank presented me with a .22 rifle and five hundred rounds of ammunition. Not, perhaps, very symbolic of peace on earth, but that was not something that concerned any of us at the time. My cup ran over, though I would not have put it like that. I blazed away at everything I saw, but I seldom hit anything – I was too excited. The most promising targets, the baboons which came as near the camp as they dared and sat and swore at us, were taboo; 'protected', I was told, because they were rare, which seemed silly to me. There seemed to be hundreds of them. Anyway, we were within the bounds of the Serengeti game reserve, as it then was, where all animals were protected. Even though we were 'two hundred miles from the nearest human habitation', you never knew where the game wardens might be. Strictly, we were only supposed to shoot 'for the pot'. On the whole, I think we kept to the rules – except for the zebra; and Father justified that by saying he was only helping nature do what it was going to do anyway.

Sometimes we would venture deep into the reserve to look at game – great browsing giraffe staring at us with their huge, heavy-lashed eyes over the tops of trees; sinister, silent herds of buffalo, black and tightly packed in the shade of an acacia, quite still except for their tails and the swarm of tick-birds keeping the parasites at bay; great masses of zebra and wilde-beast, either grazing or swinging away in panic with their silly falsetto barks as we approached; ostriches, cheetahs and every kind of antelope; as well as warthogs, monkeys and many smaller animals. And everywhere, circling expectantly, the inevitable vultures, waiting for the predators to let them clear up their leavings. Birds, of course, and butterflies in exuberant plenty. African game country is now familiar to everyone through countless films and documentaries, but in the thirties it was really unknown to all but a few; for ten days we did not see any sign of another human being. This was a proper safari.

We did not catch sight of elephant or rhino, though we heard one of the latter crashing about near the camp one night, and snorting crossly. It was quite frightening, actually, because Father, in his usual way, sat with his powerful .318 sporting rifle at the ready, saying things like: 'He's coming this way,' and 'Brace yourselves, I think he's caught our scent – he'll charge if he does.' Fortunately, the rhino, having dropped a huge turd (which we excitedly examined the next day) ambled away, and the night settled down to the mad hyena laughter and the squeaky-door calls of the hyrax in the tall trees by the stream. And the occasional grunt of the lion.

We saw a lion once. It was a huge handsome male with a great dark mane, sitting by itself in the shade of an inevitable flat-topped acacia thorn. We bumped off the road – insanely, I thought – to within a hundred and fifty yards of him. He sat and watched us coldly. It must be remembered that the game were not yet used to inquisitive motor cars as they are today, so I suppose I was right to be scared; we were being a bit foolhardy. Father again had his .318 at the ready (my little .22 was firmly kept from my reach. 'That thing would only make him angry.') When the lion stood up and stretched Father said, hardly moving his lips, 'Watch his tail; if it straightens out, he's coming.' Sure enough, he stuck his tail straight out behind him, and my bowels became very uncertain. The tension was enormous. Everyone was absolutely still. The moment stretched and stretched. I could swear that I could see his terrifying yellow eyes picking me out as the tenderest morsel. Then he shot a stream of pee onto the ground, yawned, and strolled calmly away into some thick scrub nearby. I think Father was quite disappointed, but Mummy said quietly, 'Drive on, Geoff, I think we've seen all we're going to.' I said, 'I want to do ishy.'

One early evening Frank had taken some of us out to get a guinea fowl for supper. We came across a flock near a waterhole and, as they rose into the air at our approach, Frank brought one down with his shotgun from the driver's seat. Before the bird hit the ground, there was a great flapping of wings, and an eagle grabbed it and tried to lumber off with it in his talons. 'You boogger,' said Frank quietly in his thick Yorkshire voice, and brought it down with his second barrel.

The eagle was winged, but not killed, and stood, angry and proud, over the guinea fowl it had plundered.

'Finish him off, Nibby,' said Frank, and I blazed away with my Christmas present – trying, of course, to hit its angry, swaying head. I never came near to hitting it and finally Frank said gently, ' 'Ere, give 'er to me.' And finished the eagle off with a single merciful shot. I have felt badly about this since. That eagle deserved to get away with its brilliant improvisatory snatch. In those days it did not occur to many people to think like that.

When we returned with our guinea fowl, we found Mummy a bit worried. Pop had wandered off somewhere by himself, promising to be back in half an hour. It would soon be dark – very suddenly once the sun has set – and he was experienced enough in the bush not to have forgotten the rules: you don't hang about when the big cats start thinking about dinner.

We all set off up the hill in the direction Father had taken, and not long afterwards we heard a distant commotion – a lot of barking mixed with some pretty pithy English invective. Half laughing and half frowning, Frank led off at a trot towards the altercation.

After a few hundred yards we came across an extraordinary spectacle. In a circle round a small tree were about fifty baboons, barking and snarling and slowly closing in on the tree. Up the tree, swinging gently back and forth by his trousers from one of the branches, Father was waving his arms about and issuing a stream of disgusting orders. The baboons were not taking kindly to this, and edged a bit nearer. Frank let out a snort of laughter, and fired his shotgun in the air, just as the sentinel baboon caught sight of us. A ring of startled faces turned towards us for a moment, and then the whole family took to its heels, and made off into its rocky fastness at the top of the hill. Leaving Father still swinging impotently back and forth. 'Get me off this bloody thing,' he shouted to us, rather hoarse by now; and we managed to lower him gently to the ground. Our laughter did not improve his humour.

He had set off, he told us, with a butterfly net, for a bit of a stroll and had seen something he wanted to catch. Without looking where he was going, he had hobbled after it up the hill, till he lost it in the tops of some trees near the summit. Then, feeling the call of nature, he had settled down in a comfortable crouch, to be confronted by a very cross baboon, baring its teeth and barking at him. As Father was now well inside his territory, he was hardly to be blamed.

Without having time to do more than haul up his pants, Father shinned up a neighbouring tree, slipped and was caught on a sticking-out branch by the seat of his trousers. The sight must have disconcerted them, for the baboons were hesitant to set about him, as they might well have done, since he was a trespasser on their home ground. Instead, they ringed the tree and swore at him, while deciding what line to take. Father, unable to pull himself back into a more dignified position, swore back – luridly – on the sensible ground that attack was the only form of defence.

'Where the hell have you been?' he said, rather than asked. He did not seem in the least grateful for being rescued. Our faces only made it worse. 'What's so bloody funny?' Again, it was a statement. Indeed, he was never quite able to see the funny side of the episode. Neither, it must be said, did the baboons. We left them sitting on their rocks, screaming at us, and making abortive little charges in our direction, just to show us what they *could* have done. That evening's sundowner, I am sure, did not come any too soon. But even Mummy laughed.

All too soon it was time to pack up camp and head for home. I was selfishly convinced that the only reason for this was because term was soon to start again, and it did not seem a sufficient one; grown-ups, however, are unstoppable. Once it starts, the juggernaut has to roll.

But this time there was a reprieve of sorts. As we approached the sandy river bed which we had bumped dustily over on our way out, there was a roaring sound and, rounding the corner, we came across an angry torrent foaming over some rocks to our right, and completely blocking the road.

Father braked to a standstill and swore under his breath. Frank, who had pulled up behind, came and leaned on the car door. 'I thought I'd seen rain in the hills,' he said, and they both turned their heads and looked bleakly at some heavy dark clouds away to the east. I was delighted. For once we were stuck, and I did not mind. School was on the other side of that brown swirling barrier, and it could go on swirling for ever as far as I was concerned.

In fact, we were only held up for three days. Rainstorms in the hills often caused flash floods, which subsided as quickly as they rose; nevertheless, twice, just as the men were deciding that in an hour or so we would be able to ford the stream to safety, there was a rumble of thunder in the distance, and before the hour was up a fresh brown swirl would top up the level again, making a crossing unthinkable.

The camp was necessarily makeshift, because we needed to be able to pack up and leave at a moment's notice. But it was quite a satisfactory spot: great slabs of rock made excellent tables, and the cars and tents made a snug kind of lager, in the open, not too near the thick vegetation which could be hiding we knew not what.

For here we did get lions round the camp, so we always kept a large fire going through the night to make them keep their distance. I may be imagining it, but I seem to remember one night, when the grunts got a bit too close for comfort, someone turned on the car headlamps suddenly, and there was a pair of gleaming eyes in the beam, just momentarily, and a tawny-coloured smear veered off into the dark. Those eyes seemed a long way apart; they must have been embedded in an enormous head. It is a very vivid memory, and I hope that it really happened.

However, none of us got eaten, and early one morning, before the rising equatorial sun could throw long dark shadows from every blade of grass, we hurriedly loaded everything up and, with our hearts in our mouths, we splashed across the dwindling river, and chugged with relief up the opposite bank.

We camped that night not very far from the sand river on an open piece of plain that swept gently downhill towards a distant ridge. There seemed to be no game anywhere, and it looked to me utterly safe, almost domestic. It was at this camp that I received one of the very few severe roastings that I had from Father. What happened was that the next morning, very early, before anyone was stirring, I heard something snuffling around outside the tents, and popping my head out of the side of the car where I slept, I saw a little fox-like animal, all white, with large bat ears and a bushy tail. I had never seen anything like it before, and thought it would make an excellent trophy. Still in my pyjamas, I collected my little rifle and some bullets and climbed out of the car without waking anyone.

The little creature had trotted about a hundred yards off and stood looking back at me, its big ears erect. As I raised my rifle to my shoulder, it took to its heels and ran off, stopping some way away to look back at me again. Too far for a shot, so I followed it. When I reckoned it was within range again, I stopped and took aim. It immediately took off again, stopping just out of range. I duly followed, and the process was repeated several times, till I was a good half-mile from the camp. I was so concentrated on my prey, I looked neither to right nor left.

Eventually I lost patience and let off a shot, missed the target and the little fox-whatever-it-was finally disappeared down its burrow. As I prepared to investigate, I heard a shot and a shout behind me, and looked round to see Father hobbling towards me, waving his arms and yelling. I walked back towards him, eager to tell him of my odd discovery, only to be greeted with an anger I had never had directed at me before. I could not understand what all the fuss was about, except that I had broken a camp rule, never to stray too far away by myself. But it was open country, we were now well out of the Serengeti, and it all seemed perfectly safe. One of my sisters said later that they had seen a hyena showing interest, but it was not until many years later that I suddenly realized why Father had reacted as he had, and my blood ran cold. Hyenas specialize in picking off young stragglers, and I must have seemed exactly that. The thought of that stinking breath and those terrifying jaws has since made me wake up in a cold sweat, but at the time I was only bewildered that my hunt had been frustrated so near its goal. And I never did discover what the animal was.

Back at Kiefie's it was time again for the ghastly business of going back to school; the tears, the gloomy packing of trunks, and the bleak early morning departure on the Goldfield Transport bus, heading for Clarissa Roberts and her runny cream, stinging ears from the attentions of Philip Abrahams, and the prospect of crying myself to sleep in the only piece of privacy available – bed.

This time, however, school became easier. I realized that Philip Abrahams had departed for the Prince of Wales School outside Nairobi. This was worth several sighs of relief, but there was more. Departed, also, was gloomy, sickly Mr Barton, with his sad, malaria-yellow eyes. In his place we were greeted by Mr Woods, dapper and crisp, with a balding shiny head and clipped moustache, and an apparently permanent blazer and crisp khaki shorts. I liked the look of him. School suddenly seemed less threatening.

Even better news was to follow. The clarion-like Clarissa had gone too. I could not believe it. For about a week I expected to wake up to her hectoring tones, but eventually I came to understand that gentle, soft-voiced Mrs Chandler, who could see no good reason for having to eat bread and cream every other day, was not just a temporary stopgap, but was there to stay. Life was definitely looking up.

During this first term of 1936 a couple of us boys were summoned to a classroom during break, sat down with a sheet of paper in front of us, and told to give a specimen of handwriting. I am left-handed, and pushing those old sharp nibs was something of an adventure. My specimen looked for all the world like a rudimentary Gerald Scarfe cartoon – all spots and splashes, where my nib had jumped and skittered across the page. Nobody told me what it was for. I handed it in apologetically, and thought no more about it.

A few weeks later I was informed that I was to catch a train to Nairobi, the capital, for an interview with the colony's director of education. It had, I was told, something to do with going to school in England, but the prospect of my first ever railway journey made everything else become of very minor importance. I was the only one from Kitale to be summoned, so I did not connect it in any way with my spluttery hand-writing specimen. A grown-up (I cannot remember who – my brother Dick, perhaps?) accompanied me; we caught the train at Eldoret for the overnight trip; and I faintly remember being treated as rather special cargo. I think I thought it was some kind of reward for good work, but otherwise I accepted it without too much surprise.

The back of the seat in each compartment lifted up at night to make the top bunk of a two-bunk cabin, and I climbed up to bed on the top soon after we left Eldoret and, when I woke up very early the next morning and peered out of the window, I could see that we were high up in some sort of hills. It was very cold and misty. I could see the railway line we had been on curling round and round on itself like a snake and the two big tank engines at the front were puffing out enormous clouds of steam as they laboured up to the top of what I now know was the great Mau Escarpment, where, past Timboroa, the line starts to curl and waver round and round again, down to the bottom of the Rift Valley at Nakuru, with its flamingo-fringed lake. It is very beautiful. The line then chugs through dusty farmland, where the earth glints invit-ingly with fool's gold in the sun, past Naivasha and the dramatic extinct volcano of Longonot, till it rises again in curves and whorls up the Ngong Escarpment out of the Rift to the Nairobi plateau at the top.

I had been to Nairobi before, and recognized its wide streets and tall banks and hotels – Torr's, the Norfolk and the New Stanley – standing proudly in their own grounds. What I had not taken in before was the imposing (not to say pompous) grandeur of Government House, all white walls and cool, arched verandahs, representing the panoply of colonial power. I was taken, wide-eyed and strange, along cool corridors by soft-footed servants in fezzes and long white robes, and ushered into the director of education's office – he could have been the governor, or God, as far as I knew. It was a huge room, and I remember two large pink-faced gentlemen staring at me benignly from behind an enormous desk. Nobody asked me whether or not I wanted to go to England; in fact, I cannot recall England ever being mentioned. It may have been, of course, my recollections of the whole interview are sketchy in the extreme; but I have no recollection of feeling that those two round Dickensian gentlemen in their white suits held my fate in their hands. I think I was put into a room by myself for a while to do a few sums; but not for a moment did I have the feeling that my life would never be the same again. Kitale School, when I returned to it, was as solid and permanent and unremitting as ever.

It was this hard outline, I think, which lay at the heart of my casual feelings about it all. England, I knew, was supposed to be soft and rather weedy, not really to be taken seriously as somewhere actually to live. Real life was led in a hard tropical light, not in a kind of underwater dream-world of chintzy drawing rooms and lace curtains, which was the impression I had received from my sisters. Life as I knew it was abundant and competitive – and cheap; not rarified and delicate and cosy. It sounded very nice, but it was merely a pretty fantasy.

That I had to look at England differently when I got there took some time to sink in. It was an England where people took distance very seriously and built fences round their houses because neighbours lived just on the other side. Here I was, and I was not to go back to real life for the foreseeable future; and England was solid, no softer than where I had come from; and the dripping winter fields round Allesley dripped neither milk nor honey. Africa, often hard and ungiving, had been my permanence, the yardstick against which I measured my toughness and self-reliance. England was supposed to be pliant and tractable: a teatime place – not for serious matters like dinner and getting run over. Yet when I slipped and fell on the icy bricks by the back door the ground was just as ungiving.

One of the solidities that most surprised me at first – apart from the cold and the eternal bustle – was the Church. I had always thought of religion as a kind of cloth-kit affair – something to be played with at idle moments or endured at boring school assemblies. To be sure, my mother said my prayers with me every night, but they were pretty perfunctory and always the same. My only contact with organized religion had been the old giggly service at Porgies, taken in spite of rather than for us by little pink Mr Tyree, whom Father always called padre, and, of course, those morning assemblies. Missionaries were, as I have said, figures of fun, and a volume of biblical paintings by Graeme Hole RA (which I rather enjoyed) were called 'that damn silly book' by Father. I had been baptized, and had a godfather and a godmother; but the godfather was no longer on speaking terms with us because of those cattle, and the godmother lived (and for all I know had died) in South Africa. I think she was called Mrs Molesworth, but I cannot be sure.

To find myself in a family whose life was centred round the tall parish church, where Matins every Sunday was a matter of course, and morning prayers in the study taken for granted as a daily occurrence; where the bells, which rang interminably not only on Sundays but on Thursday practice nights too, made me sympathise with Charity, the cat who hid under Bobby's bed till they stopped; and where nightly prayers with Ailie were not only varied, but an occasion for summing up the day; where Church, in fact, was not only taken seriously, but was the reason for the family being where it was; all this needed to be carefully assimilated.

I cannot say that I took to it like a duck to its pond, but I became acclimatized, and accepted it as part of this strange serious life I had to lead. A life where I had to make my bed every day, leave my room tidy, and not go out without wrapping up; a life where I stood by my chair at all meals (except tea, for some reason) until grace had been said by one or other of us (my heart was in my mouth when I was first asked to say it); and where we *did not use table napkins*. A life, moreover, where the nights were quieter than the days (though no less frightening for that; a single rustle coming out of total silence was just as terrifying as the continual howls and whistles and groans of an African night).

At the head of this family edifice was the rector – the Reverend Rupert Bede Winser – who had the cure of souls in the parish of All Saints, Allesley. Though there was never any question but that Aunt Alison was the boss, Rupert was, nevertheless, the head of the family, and needed to be reckoned with.

The rector came from a large family of devout and eccentric siblings, whose father, Charles Winser, also a clergyman, had been rector of Adderley, near Market Drayton. Charles, a gentle, misty-eyed man from his photographs, had died many years before I came within the family orbit. But his widow, Anne, known throughout her large brood of grandchildren as Grancy, was very much in evidence. By the time I came on the scene Grancy was over eighty, deaf and sprawling in huge tweed skirts and voluminous tops, and she lived in an equally sprawling house smelling of lavender, just outside the little town of Aberdovey on the coast of Merioneth. Here the entire Winser clan descended for their summer holidays, and filled the house with swimming and walking gear and ancient Ordnance Survey maps. Grancy bullied everyone with an enormous ear-trumpet, knew more about us all than we did ourselves, and was the only person I knew who managed to intimidate my Aunt Ailie. We all adored her, even her slave of a youngest daughter, Catherine, and we were made to sit beside her when we arrived at *Bryneithyn*, and yell our news into her trumpet.

Rupert, the sixth of her nine children and the gentlest, had the most execrable handwriting. This, apparently, was the outcome of a bizarre accident when he was a small boy. He was out with Grancy in the family dog-cart, and had the top of the index finger on his right hand chopped off by catching it in the wheel. Grancy, so he told me, whoaed the pony, jumped down, found the fingertip and, having blown the dust off it, clamped it back in place (roughly) and it took; though his handwriting never overcame this lumpy obstacle, at least Uncle Rupert had a full complement of fingers.

As I may have suggested already, I was never fully at ease with the rector; largely, I suspect, because he was not at ease with me. He had a kind of boy-scout exuberance with children that I had never come across before. I found it quite unnerving; I never knew what to expect. He would sometimes make exaggerated gestures, thumping one hand into the other and shouting with laughter; or he might suddenly start to wrestle, as though that was what children liked to do, but he was wrong about this child. One day, when we were walking together in the Welsh hills, while the rest of the family settled down to a picnic, he suddenly decided we should take our clothes off and *run about.* I pranced half-heartedly about the bracken, scratched and embarrassed, until he had had enough. We returned to the family amid hilarious jokes about the first pink sheep to be seen in the Principality. I was devastated, but he laughed merrily and talked about God's fresh air on our bodies.

His sermons, too, were sometimes unexpected. Preaching once about the endlessness of God's love, he illustrated his theme by telling us about seeing Niagara Falls as a young man. 'There I stood,' he declaimed, 'full of wonder – trying to *drink it all in.*' When he was teased about it afterwards, he laughed, but there was a tiny furrow of bewilderment between his brows.

And yet he was the gentlest of men. I never heard him speak a harsh word to anyone, and his kindness and generosity to me never wavered. Quite often he would suddenly say to me, 'You do know that this will always be your home for as long as you want it.' I was surprised each time; it never entered my head that anyone might have been thinking anything else.

In spite of his frequently tangled sermons, he had a beautiful speaking voice, and clearly enjoyed the stately language of *The Book of Common Prayer.* I suppose I was vaguely aware of this, but I found Matins immeasurably tedious, and quite incomprehensible. My cousin Sue, I suspect, felt much the same as I, but she was more to the manner born and knew how to dream a satisfactory way through it all. My heart always sank when we began the Venite. Ailie hooted her way through 'Ooooh, comeletussingunto the Loord, letus HEARTilyrejoice – inthe strengthofour salVA-TION'. It was quite incomprehensible. What on earth did 'forty years long was I grieved with this generation and SAID' mean? I liked the General Thanksgiving with its rolling periods: '. . . but above all for thine inestimable love in the redemption of the world by our Lord Jesus Christ'. What it *meant* I had no idea but that was the least of my worries; I didn't understand any of it, actually. However, it was good basic training and I am grateful for it.

Whichever of the boys were at home came dutifully to church, of course, but they had more sophisticated ways of dealing with Matins. They took bets on how many howlers their father would make and, standing dignified and upright in the rectory pew, exchanged expressionless looks with each other at the eccentricities of the congregation. They played sermon cricket, with an elaborate method of scoring, involving fluffs, hesitations, repetitions, and particular references, biblical and topical. Not by a flicker did they betray their feelings, except for an occasional whimper if a match was boiling up to an exciting climax. I was not supposed to know about this, and was put firmly in my place if I referred to it. Africa seemed a very long way away on such occasions.

XII

IT WAS AN ORDINARY DAILY ASSEMBLY. THE TROPICAL SUN slanted strongly through the high windows of the gallery which ran round the school hall, and motes drifted gently down the beams. We were arranged according to forms – juniors in front, seniors behind; girls on the right, boys on the left. We settled into the restless hush when the staff arrived, sang the requisite hymn and said the usual prayers. We listened demurely, with lowered eyes, to the head saying the grace, then lifted our heads and relaxed for the regular morning announcements. Mr Woods cleared his throat. The world was sailing normally on its course.

'You will be pleased to hear,' he said, 'that' – pause – 'Evans has won the scholarship to Christ's Hospital.' The world tipped slightly from its orbit. There was a short pause. I heard someone gasp – was it Tricia? Or me? Then there was a storm of clapping, my first experience of applause. Boys standing near me slapped me on the back. The world tipped further over, and I felt sort of weightless. It was quite a pleasant sensation, all this clapping, but I had no idea what to do next.

212

Mr Woods told my parents subsequently that 'Evans did not know what to do with his feet.' Tricia, of course, burst into tears. Momentous events have to fit into banal situations. If you take a heavy cold with you on the road to Samarkand, you are liable to have to share the arrival with a stuffed-up nose. I had been having a fierce discussion about what we would have for lunch before assembly began. Would this make any difference? I wondered.

England. Going to England, where life is cushy, and there aren't any snakes. England. The word began to be unrecognizable, like a foreign name. Would I have to leave my family? No-one seemed to have thought of that. It was important and I felt important. And special – like being wrapped up with ribbons. That was nice too. But scared, a bit; there was a great big unknown hole up in front; tent pegs were being pulled up all round me.

Mr Woods was kind, and laughed at my bewilderment. He let me off morning school, and my friend Jim (I think he was called) was let off too, to keep me company. Tricia gave me a damp hug and disappeared to her class. We wandered aimlessly about, and then decided to go to our classroom. School is an extraordinarily empty place when everyone but you is busy.

After this there was a pause. I knew something was going on, but no-one was telling me about it. One of my sisters told me, years later, that Mr Woods wrote proudly to my parents to give them the news, but apparently they had only entered me for the scholarship as a kind of joke and could not possibly afford to send me to England, and would have to turn it down.

Pressure was applied by various friends, and they both came to Kitale to see the headmaster. I was excited to see the old Chev rolling up unexpectedly, and both Tricia and I were very put out to find they had not come to take us out. They were both distracted – Mummy inclined to be tearful – and they went away again, and still no-one said anything to me.

I suppose that finally a decision was made, for eventually, things got moving again, and I was told that I would be leaving in a week or two, and would miss the rest of term. This was due to the sudden intervention of our neighbour from Porgies, W. J. Carter, the strange, Poirot-like half-French bachelor, who, I am now convinced, carried a torch for my mother. He promised to finance my journey to England, and it is frustrating to know that I have never been aware enough of what he did for me properly to thank him. He died many years before I was old enough to know how much I owe him.

Before I could leave Kitale, I had the strange and uncomfortable experience of having all the rest of my baby teeth extracted. I had suddenly blown up with gumboils; my face, already round, was like a balloon, and the school dentist said I should have my teeth out, particularly if I was shortly to undertake a long sea voyage. No doubt he had his own logic for this pronouncement – gumboils, after all, do get better – but in those days any kind of specialist was looked on as infallible, so out came all my teeth.

I had two sessions with that dentist. He looked like a wolf

and kept grinning widely at me; I felt a bit like Red Riding Hood. I am sure he was kindly, but it seemed a ruthless process, in the dictionary sense of unsparing. He did not use any anaesthetic, and again I am sure that there was a good reason for this; all I was aware of was that wide grin and what seemed like an enormous pair of cruel pliers, which gripped mercilessly and wrenched with a horrible crackling sound. Seven times on that first day, and six on the second. It hurt a lot, and I bled a lot, but the swellings went down miraculously, I seem to remember.

However, after the second session, there outside the surgery was Frank, ever faithful, and more like a brother to me than Dick. He had my trunk in the back of his dark green Vauxhall, which we called the Locust because it had a peculiar shape, and he had come to take me away from Kitale for ever. I had a few regrets: Mr Woods had been very kind and amusing; I had at last begun to make some friends; and I had a small pang at saying goodbye to Miss Tatham, with her 'EXCELLENT' stamps and her pretty blouses. My chief regret, though, was not being able to take part in the school play. It was going to be the mechanics' scene from A Midsummer Night's Dream and I had been cast as Starveling. All I had to do was to stand on a chair holding up a hurricane lamp on a curved pole. 'This lanthorn doth the horned moon present, and I the man in the moon do seem to be.' I had no idea what I was talking about, or what the play was about, but it seemed fun and I was sorry to miss it. My experience of live theatre was not extensive. I had been thrilled to watch The Teasing of

215

Malvolio the year before, but that was chiefly because Malvolio was played by my least favourite person, Philip Abrahams, who made my life unpleasant. It was a sheer delight to see him being twitted and reduced by Sir Toby Belch and his gang. I did not know what that play was about either, but that did not matter; I felt I was being avenged.

It was to yet another home that Frank was taking me and my tender mouth. Father had landed the job of manager of an uncertain-looking enterprise called Owombo Mines, not far beyond Kakamega, the chief mining town of north-west Kenya. I had been nodding sleepily as we drove, gingerly exploring my sore gums with my tongue. We had not talked much.

Soon after we had left Kakamega behind, Frank suddenly said, in his flat Yorkshire voice, ' 'Ere we go – hangg on to yer hat.' We rounded a sharp bend, and were immediately confronted by a deep gorge a few yards ahead. Through it the brown, swirling Yala River rushed hungrily, the trees on either side leaning right down towards the water. Spanning the gorge was a neat and tidy suspension bridge, a clever piece of engineering: a bridge made of wooden slats two or three inches apart, through which the water below could be seen. Down the length of the bridge ran two parallel plank tracks, just the width of car wheels. And that was all. There was no parapet, no railing, not even a piece of string to give the illusion of safety.

I stared at Frank, and he gave me a grin out of one side of his mouth. He slipped into low gear, and eased the Locust onto the parallel planks. Once on it, there was nothing to be seen of the bridge on either side. Frank casually nodded his head to the right. 'He didn't make it, poor devil.'

I looked in the direction of his nod, gently, so as not to rock the car. Against an angry-looking rock, with the water breaking all round it, a rusty car had been washed up. I looked back at Frank. His eyes were steady on the track ahead.

At last we bumped off the bridge, and rounded another sharp bend immediately beyond it. Frank grinned at me, his bad teeth showing. He should have stopped off at the dentist with me. 'Exciting that,' he said, and I grinned back. 'Yeah.' But all I could think of was that sooner or later I would have to cross that bridge again. The wrecked car became something of a grim symbol.

The house at Owombo seemed to me immensely smart; it had proper doors and windows with glass in them. It was one of about half-a-dozen square, ugly bungalows, built for the Europeans who worked at the mine and the mill by the river in the valley below. Ours stood on stilts because of the sloping ground, with six steps leading up to the front verandah, and a huge five-hundred gallon galvanized tank at the side to collect rainwater. The Africans' quarters – round thatched huts – were at the back among some trees where the hyraxes creaked away all night.

Under the house among the stilts it was dry and dark, and nothing could grow. It became my favourite playground. I made endless winding roads between houses and settlements, along which I could drive my two Dinky toys, visiting and trading and creating domestic dramas. Actually, one of them was a Tootsie toy, a smart Vauxhall saloon, which I had repainted a glossy blue with a white roof. The Dinky was a clapped-out red Bedford truck, and it served as taxi and transport, as well as trouble maker for the rich owners of the Vauxhall. The only disadvantage of this paradise was that I had to share it with my mother's ubiquitous chickens, which clucked and scratched out my roads for food when I was not there to chase them away. Every day I had to reconstitute the roads and put the houses to rights before I was able to pursue my story of high finance and social mayhem. I always played there by myself; the only time I showed it to another little boy who had been brought over to keep me company he insisted on building new roads and houses himself, which changed the scenario and wrecked the plot. I was happiest playing alone.

A hundred yards or so below our house was another bungalow, almost identical, but with a high euphorbia hedge all round it. The people who lived there were friendly and let me explore, but the space beneath their house was no good – the ground was not so slopey, and the stilts weren't tall enough. It was dank and uncomfortable – and I found a snake there. The previous occupiers must, as Father said enigmatically, have been fond of lifting the elbow, for behind the house was a mountain of empty bottles. I discovered that I could get a few cents for each one if I took them to the big general store in Kisumu, and the people in the house were only too pleased to be relieved of them. So every time I went into Kisumu with my parents, I took a dozen or so bottles and flogged them to the Indian storekeeper. I was kept comfortably in pocket money until I left for England and was even able to lend Tricia ready cash when she needed it. As she was then fifteen and getting interested in cosmetics, she was always short. I lent her the money at interest and did a roaring trade.

In Kisumu, behind one of the bigger trading posts, was a delicious dry rubbish dump, where all the old envelopes and postal wrappings were thrown. I was allowed to forage for stamps among this great heap of paper, and was kept happily occupied for as long as the grown-ups were busy. I built a handsome collection of British and East African stamps.

I left Kitale in June, and sailed for England on 24 October, so I was at Owombo for nearly four months, the longest time I had been anywhere since we had left Porgies and I was happy on the whole, though the looming void of my departure was always there ahead. What it must have been like for my mother I only learnt when I had children of my own. Father, I think, was rather more sanguine. Easy-come-easy-go, he had a cheerful, uncomplicated view of life, which took little account of the dark or fearful side of things. Many years later I said jokingly to my eldest sister Marion, 'I expect he was glad to have one less mouth to feed.' She looked coolly at me. 'Well, of course,' she said. 'What else would you expect?' And I remember once hearing him talk about the threat to North Africa of Mussolini's expansionist ambitions (this was 1936, the year Italy invaded Abyssinia). He turned my blood to ice for a moment when he chuckled and said, 'My God, if there's a war up there, you won't see me for dust.' Which is indeed what he did; when the war broke out three years later, he lied about his age (he was fifty-nine), enlisted, and disappeared into the mountains of Abyssinia as soon as he could tie his bootlaces. My mother made no comment, then or later. She was an endurer.

One of the men who worked at Owombo Mines with Father was a cheerful rogue called Pat. He had an attractive crooked smile full of gold teeth, a snazzy two-seater, and an eye for the girls. As there were at least two available and quite pretty girls in our house at any one time, we saw a good deal of Pat. I liked him – in fact, he became something of a hero to me after he saved me from a huge African rather the worse for drink, who was threatening me with my own .22 rifle. I was paralysed with terror until Pat, who happened to come by, made short work of rescuing me. I was overwhelmed that someone who a moment before had been so frightening could be reduced to cringing apology from a few crisp words. Pat gave me back my gun with a flash of gold teeth and told me not to be scared. That was how I wanted to be when I grew up.

One day Pat announced that they were showing Charlie Chaplin's film *Modern Times* in Kakamega, and offered to take us all to see it. There was not enough room in his little car, so we used Dick's battered old Chev which, when it had belonged to Frank, had come with us on safari the Christmas before. We all piled in – Pat, Dick, two of the girls and I – and lumbered off towards Kakamega.

Of course, we had to cross my dread bridge to get there and

Pat managed it with great skill. However, I knew that it now lay between me and my little bed at Owombo, which some-what coloured my evening.

Modern Times was only the second film I had seen. The first was *The Gay Divorcee*, with Astaire and Rogers, some time before in Kitale. I had been about five, and took in very little. This one I loved, particularly the bit where Charlie is tightening an everlasting line of nuts with a huge spanner. So automatic did his tightening movements become that, when a ravishing blonde walked by, he calmly tightened both her breasts. I felt very grown-up and joined in heartily with the audience's laughter.

When it was over I was put blearily to sleep in the back of the car, wrapped in Mummy's ubiquitous fur coat, while the others had what they called a quick drink.

I woke up when they returned to the car, and immediately began to worry about the bridge. This was not allayed by the sight of Pat climbing tipsily into the driving seat, singing cheerfully and crashing gears as we swerved out of the car park. Nobody else seemed to be worried, but I wonder now if I was the only one who could think of nothing but those two parallel planks. We wove merrily out of the town into the dark countryside.

Suddenly the headlights failed, and I sent up a prayer of thanks. It was very dark; that was it. Pull up and let's all go to sleep. Then my brother produced a torch, and held it outside the car. 'Can you see, Pat?' 'Course – clear as day,' sang Pat, and we wove on. I knew in a flash what drove people to murder. No-one mentioned the bridge. They all seemed to be singing, 'Show me the way to go home . . .' I thought of the rusty skeleton wrapped round the rocks in that ravine. I crouched down in the folds of my mother's coat. Pat speeded up.

All of a sudden there was a lurch and I felt myself flying through the air, still clutching Mummy's fur coat. I immediately thought that we had come off the bridge, but then I bounced on the ground and looked up, winded, to see the car's front wheels silhouetted against the sky. 'Blimey. What a bumpy road,' came Pat's cheerful voice from the darkness. 'Everyone all right?' I did not care; all I could think was, We'll not be crossing the bridge tonight. By not very surprising good fortune, Pat had missed a curve in the road and driven into a storm drain.

Actually, none of us was hurt at all; even the car was not as badly damaged as it deserved to be. Some passing Indians picked us out of the ditch, and took us back into Kakamega where someone found us beds. I have no further memory of the escapade, for I was so relieved at not having to cross that bridge, I fell asleep and did not stir till someone woke me with breakfast. We were driven home. For some reason, negotiating the bridge no longer held any fears for me, and I never worried about it again.

I did not seem any longer to be able to make friends with the African *totos*, perhaps school had Anglicized me too much. There was always a restraint between us which had never been there at Porgies. But, with Tricia home from school, we could play the camel-hair rope game together again. One of us was blindfolded by the other and pulled around at the end of the rope into the most awkward hazards we could find, amid hilarious laughter. I suppose the reason why we were never attacked by snakes was that we were making so much noise, blundering about and shrieking, that any self-respecting snake would make itself scarce well before we came anywhere near it.

Another dangerous ploy which I developed was to commandeer one of the heavy metal wheelbarrows from the mine and broom-broom about with it, usually on the run, finding all kinds of hazards and difficult routes to negotiate. I found this an endlessly delightful pastime, and no-one, to my knowledge, told me how dangerous it was. The wheelbarrow had hollow iron handles, unguarded by any covering. Of course, what happened was inevitable. I was tearing along a path and came across a hidden rock. The wheelbarrow stopped more quickly than I did, and the hollow handle went into my left shin. Surprisingly, I was not badly hurt, but there was a lot of blood, and I made quite a fuss. I have a circular scar on my shin to this day.

Luckily for me, my mother put an enormous bandage on my leg, and this probably saved it, for about a week later, on a walk with one of my sisters past the mine shaft, I climbed up to the pithead and began to push one of the heavy trolleys that carried away the mine spoil. The trolley was on a kind of railway and I assumed, as I speeded up, that there was a buffer at the end to stop it. There wasn't. Clinging to the heavy iron trolley as it rolled over and fell to the jumbled rocks below all took place in slow motion. I cannot say that I enjoyed it, but it was exciting, though I should by rights have been squashed flat. Actually I fell beneath the trolley and landed between two large quartz boulders. These stopped the trolley's fall, and it ended upside down, with the edge a couple of inches from my face. It teetered for a moment and the far corner finally settled – on my heavily bandaged leg.

My sister Dorothy who was with me claimed that if I had stopped screaming at that point she would have fainted; but I did not stop, and she did not faint, but called for help instead. I suppose it was not long before some people came and eased the trolley off my leg so that I could scramble out, still yelling, but somewhat chastened when I looked back to where I had been. I was very lucky; even my bandage had come to my aid for, though the sharp corner had cut right through it, I only had one more unattractive bloody hole, instead of a mangled leg. So I now have two scars on my shin, which have been 'distinguishing marks' in my passport and my AB64 army paybook.

As a result of these misadventures, I left for England with a heavily bandaged left leg, for my departure was only a week or so away. The threat of departure at last had to be taken seriously. Suddenly the ground under my feet seemed very uncertain, and I would be disconcerted to find Mummy dashing away a tear as she stood over the kitchen stove.

She became uncharacteristically querulous, too. I had a friend from school whom I did not like very much, called

Maurice. He lived within striking distance of Owombo, and we went over to his parents' house one day, because they were old acquaintances of my parents. On the way home in the car, as I was hoping that we would get to Owombo before dark so that I could go and play on my own for a bit – Maurice was all right, I suppose, but we did not have the same ideas about toys, and, anyway, he did not really like me playing with his, I could tell – I heard my mother say, 'I could kill that woman. I was saying how much I was dreading Nibby going, and do you know what she said?' She mimicked the lady cruelly. ' "Yes, I *know*, I'm simply *hating* the thought of Maurice going back to school." ' My mother's voice became almost frenzied. 'Nibby's going to be away for *seven years*.' Father chuckled and patted her knee. 'Now then, old thing, don't get so worked up; you know quite well what a silly arse she is.' Tears of rage and self-pity were coursing down Mummy's cheeks.

Seven years. It meant little to me; I could easily understand how Maurice's mother felt; one term at Kitale or seven years in England seemed much the same to me. Perhaps if I had known that I would not see my mother or Africa again for twenty years, and Father never, it might have had more impact, but I doubt it. At ten, parting is for ever anyway, so why quibble about time?

Nevertheless, the dread was mingled with excitement as my luggage began to accumulate, and I was kitted out with new clothes. Apart from my school uniform, which did not really count, these were the first bought clothes I had ever possessed. All my clothes hitherto had been run up on my mother's overworked Singer and, though they were perfectly adequate, they were hardly bespoke tailoring. It was quite a thing. Particularly a smart grey suit and overcoat, and a matching wide-brimmed felt terai hat of which I was inordinately proud. The fact that the suit and coat were pitifully unsuited to an English winter, and the hat was to attract gleeful pointings in Oxford Street, was not something to which anyone had given thought. On my last day I was snapped from every conceivable angle (so long as my bandage did not show) and I, in turn, took photographs of the family standing on the steps of the bungalow. Copies of these were sent after me to England, and were to cause not a few tears when they arrived several weeks later at Allesley.

Actually, I could have done with that hat the following summer. I was very scornful of the pale English sun and refused to wear a sunhat for games, and, to my shame, went down with sunstroke for the first time in my short life. The little boys in their first year were thought not to be quite ready for cricket and we played an odd game called Stoolball, which I think is indigenous to Sussex. I loved it. It was a variant of cricket and was played with a tennis ball and a kind of ping-pong bat. The wickets looked like notice boards at the top of a tall pole and the bowler, if my memory serves me right, stood between the – were they called 'stools'? – and bowled under-arm. Like cricket, it entailed the fielding side spending a good deal of time in the field, waiting for the ball to come one's way. It was while fielding on a lovely June day that I suddenly keeled over, feeling sick and dizzy. When I opened my eyes I seemed to be looking at the world through the wrong end of a telescope.

I was carried over to the school infirmary, somewhat baldly known as the Sicker, and had my first encounter with Dr Friend, the school doctor. He had the looks and mannerisms of Lionel Barrymore, who played, I think, the doctor in the Andy Hardy films: a great deal of bark, and some pretty crisp diagnoses, but no bite at all – though I must admit that it took me several years to find this out. I was all of seventeen when I did, and had been asked to produce a specimen for my army medical. I attended morning surgery, armed with my little bottle and handed it to Dr Friend when I was summoned to his presence. He took it from me and went over to a cupboard, and poured some sort of chemical into it and shook it up. He looked at it for a moment, put it down on his desk and stared at me over his spectacles. He was a daunting personality, and I quailed a bit.

'Well, Evans,' he said finally. 'I hope it was fun.'

I was baffled, and must have looked it. He flicked a thumb at my specimen. I followed his gesture with my eyes. The bottle of liquid had gone all milky. I was alarmed. Had I developed some fell disease? I looked back at him uncertainly.

He raised an eyebrow, then roared with laughter.

'Don't look so scared – there's nothing wrong with you. We've all done it, you know – and it won't make you go blind, or grow hairs on the palms of your hands.'

For a moment I was puzzled, and then I blushed. My little

solitary nocturnal misdemeanour had been found out. I sat transfixed. Would I get reported and beaten?

He smiled gently at me, the brusque tyrant quite gone. 'It's all right,' he said. 'It won't hurt you. But go easy; and it's not a good idea before matches – puts your eye out.'

From that day I was his slave.

That first sojourn in the Sicker did not last long. I was a healthy little boy, and my body soon mended itself, but I had never been ill away from my mother before – apart from seasickness – and I missed her badly. The school infirmary was well run and kindly, but the object was to get the boys back to school as quickly as possible. There was no gentle convalescence with guinea-fowl sandwiches and tinned pears. It was back to one's house, with a pass to say one was excused games, and that was it. As being on a pass was fairly boring – intentionally, I am sure – it paid to get back to fitness as soon as maybe. For a time, I felt a little bleak.

As I said, those photographs were taken on my last day at home. Tricia, my closest sibling, had bidden me a tearful farewell some weeks before, as she made her solitary way back to Kitale, and now it was my turn.

On the night before I left, I was allowed to sleep in my parents' bed. It did not make for a peaceful night.

In fact, Father became quite cross, because every time I stopped crying Mummy started, which started me off again, and so on, throughout the night. Father groaned, and pulled the covers over his head, but I do not think he had any better a night than we did.

The train left Kisumu in the early afternoon. Mummy and Father took me to the station. On the way we stopped at a shop to buy two packets of cream crackers and a pound of butter. That is what I had chosen to eat during the train journey to the coast. The coast. I had not seen the sea since I was three months old, so even this was to be a new experience. There was a strange feeling of unreality. At any moment I would wake from this odd dream. My parents saw me to my compartment, and sat down on either side of me. There was a funny little fat man opposite, who smiled at them and said he would keep an eye on me. I felt quite detached.

Then I remember that the guard's whistle blew, and the spell was broken. I followed them desperately as they left the compartment, stepped down onto the platform, closed the door. I was holding both their hands, as the engine gave a screech, and with a loud chuff-chuff-chuff, the train started to move. The increasing speed tore our hands apart, and I was leaning, crying, out of the window, my arm outstretched, not waving, but imploring.

The two shabby figures on the platform, one small and round and bareheaded, the other tall and erect and rather gaunt in his pith helmet, grew smaller and smaller, till I could no longer see them through my tears. I stumbled back to the compartment to be greeted by the rotund little man who had been sitting opposite. He offered me a cup of tea from his thermos. It tasted salty from the tears that by now were everywhere.

He was called Mr Tompkins and he had a shiny, pink,

well-filled face and, as far as I can remember, the only care he took of me on the trip was to insist that I took a large dose of Eno's before breakfast the next morning. He was jolly, and I am sure he did his best to cheer me up. He cannot have had a very exciting journey.

Jimmy Mactear and his German wife Gerda met the train at Mombasa, and I felt very important. Jimmy was police commissioner, or something, and he looked very handsome and reassuring in his immaculate white uniform. He had a small pencil moustache and looked like Errol Flynn, and, as Gerda was a pretty, Jessie Matthews type with sticking out teeth and a Eugene wave, they made a glamorous couple. Their wedding up country a couple of years before had been something of a social event, and we had all been thrilled when Jimmy had promised to see me onto the boat.

They made a great fuss of me, and as a special treat that afternoon they were going to take me for a sail in their yacht. I had never seen the sea before and found the horizon bewildering. The horizons I knew were not flat and endless like this, there was always a mountain or a hill – at least a tree – to break the line. Also, Lake Victoria was the biggest stretch of water I had so far seen, and it did not have waves as big as these. When I was told that we were all going to set off in the tiny shell that was bouncing and lurching about – even in harbour – I thought they had gone mad. But worse was to come. The sail was put up, and we leaned gently over till we reached the open sea, when the damn thing tilted over at a really alarming angle, and everyone sat on the opposite side, with their bottoms over the open water, as if to stop the whole thing turning turtle. I was terrified. Of course, I could not swim, and there had been a lot of hearty badinage about how shark-infested the waters of Mombasa were. The whole operation seemed totally idiotic to me, and I crouched gibbering on the bottom boards, impervious to the exhortations of my hosts, who seemed to be thoroughly enjoying their last moments. I don't think the Mactears thought much of me, and were, I am sure, greatly relieved to see me onto the ship that evening. I have never sailed since, and my heart still quails when I see a little boat keel over as it hits the wind out of harbour.

The Dunluce Castle was not, by any stretch of the imagination, a great liner. She was of some 11,000 tons, and had seen many years service on the round-Africa route. Her decks were white with age and her rails thick with countless layers of paint. But to me she was huge: a great slab of mauve wall against the dockside, stretching endlessly to right and left, and up to the skies. Little figures could be seen staring down from above, and a steep and narrow gangway led up into the mysterious insides. I climbed in gingerly, and found myself on a long solid covered way, with doors and windows on one side and the cranes and warehouses of Mombasa harbour on the other. A warm smell of food and smoke and oil came wafting out of the open doors.

The Mactears saw me to my cabin. As we passed the saloon, the smell of drink joined the others in a mixture I was to get to know intimately. My cabin was down below, deep in the

231

tourist section – could it once have been called steerage? – and, even tied up in harbour, there was the ever-present throb of the engines and the smell of hot pipes took over from the other ones up top.

My luggage was already there when I arrived – an old black Army and Navy tin trunk, flecked with red, which had been part of Father's baggage when he left England for South Africa at the turn of the century. It had a wooden lining rather the worse for termites, and strong metal clasps which you pulled down over hooks to keep it shut. No-one had got round to putting a padlock on it, with predictable results later.

Not only had my luggage preceded me, so, too, had my travelling companion; and he had already unpacked his enormous bottle of Eno's. He gave me a jolly greeting, as if he had known all along that we were to travel together, and Jimmy and Gerda Mactear were clearly relieved that we knew each other, for they made their escape quite quickly and scuttled off back to the security of the shore. I found myself alone with the merry Mr Tompkins and his Eno's. He had already commandeered the bottom bunk.

I was nominally in the care of a couple called Petrie, farmers from near Porgies, who had made, I think, a packet from marketing passion-fruit juice. But they were travelling first class and between us was a great gulf fixed, which I was far too timid to try and bridge. As they obviously did not fancy slumming, I saw hardly anything of them on the four-week voyage. This, I found, bothered me hardly at all. Colonel Petrie was a tiny wiry man with an aggressive moustache, who looked like a jockey, while Mrs P. was large and tall, with thick arms and a horsy voice. I recall Father making a coarse joke to do with horse-riding about them, which I did not understand, but which was greeted with gales of laughter. Actually, they were a kindly couple, but, as they had no children, we found little common ground. I suspect that they were only too relieved to leave me to the tender mercies of Mr Tompkins and his Eno's.

That first night on board was not easy. The stewardess was kind and helpful, but I was very shy and homesick, and stayed in my cabin. I had taken one look at the dining room and fled in terror. I broached my packet of cream crackers, but I must have sat on them, for they were seriously crumbly, and my butter had gone all runny. I was hungry, though, so I made what I could of them.

We must have set sail after my bedtime, because I was suddenly aware of much more urgent throbbing from the engines, and hissings and bangings and creakings. Then I became aware of an extremely unpleasant motion, which made my insides feel peculiar. Funnily enough, no-one had warned me about seasickness; I simply thought I was dying. Mr Tomkins laughed (I cannot think why seasickness is regarded as a joke), and offered me a glass of Eno's, but it fizzed in my throat and came straight back. He then told me to lie down, and wisely left the cabin. The smells of the ship became a touch invasive.

When daylight came we were spanking along in a stiff breeze. The stewards laughed when I said it was rough, but it was rough enough for me. There was no sign of land when I peered through the porthole, and I was told firmly not to try and open it. I saw the reason for this when the cabin went dark green and water sloshed against it a moment later. They laughed again when I told them we were sinking, but then bright sunshine flooded the cabin as the old ship hauled herself out of the swell. Nothing mattered much; I was feeling so ghastly that death would have come as a welcome release.

I did finally manage to drag myself as far as the dining room. – 'What you need, young man, is some good food inside you.' – But the staircase was alternately vertical and horizontal, and this, combined with the rich mixture of lunch, oil and the ever-present whiff of alcohol, completed my rout, and I retreated in disorder.

This state of affairs went on for about a century until we rounded the Horn of Africa, and came into relatively sheltered water. I dared to creep up on deck, and stare at the distant flat brown of the African coast, and experienced, for the first time, the incredible brightness and clarity of a ship at sea. And I was finally given some good advice. I was assured that the weather we had been through was mild for the Indian Ocean, but I marvelled that the old Dunluce Castle had survived such a buffeting. Everyone else I met on board was obviously an experienced traveller, and knew well the difference between a heavy swell and a force nine gale, so my misery was merely a source of amusement.

I was very lonely those first days on the Dunluce. Everything I knew I had left behind, and what lay ahead was a looming cloud of uncertainty. I saw the Petries just once, when we reached Aden; but, by this time, I had made a friend. I shall come to that in a moment.

The anchorage at Aden was surrounded by little boats full of Arabs offering baskets and rugs and trips round the harbour or to a sister. The ship was mercifully still, and I was leaning intrigued over the side watching it all when I was summoned to the Petrie cabin, and invited to go ashore with them and some friends to see the sights. I could not think of a good enough reason for refusing, so off we bobbed in a perilous little boat towards the rather grim, fort-like ochre seafront.

The friends were an enormous couple who said they knew my parents; very jolly and sporty and military. They were called Grantully, I think, and the husband and Colonel Petrie had clearly served together in the war, and the two huge wives honked chattily to each other. They were as friendly as they could be to me, but it must have been something of a duty chore for them, for we had very little in common. After a tour of – I suppose – the souk, we repaired to the biggest hotel for lunch. I felt very spare, and became fascinated by the punkah-wallah who sat, apparently fast asleep, with a piece of string attached to one big toe. This string activated the punkah, a large sort of pelmet hanging from the ceiling, which swung back and forth stirring the sluggish air when the punkah-wallah moved his foot. He did this seemingly without waking up. He must have been relieved from time to time, but we were there for about two hours, and the punkah never stopped punking.

That is all I remember about Aden, except that Mr –
Colonel? Major? – Grantully made loud and jocular remarks
for my benefit about how much he had been thrashed at his
public school in England, the idea being, I imagine, that
thrashing would prove to be the making of a shy, silent little
boy.

This, I was to discover, was a subject that English middle-
class men loved to talk about to small boys. 'A good hiding'
seemed to be the mainstay of British education, to judge from
the way the phrase was bandied about. One of Duff's friends in
Leamington, an otherwise gentle creature who suffered from
what I now suppose to have been multiple sclerosis, but which
was then called creeping paralysis, once surprised me by
asking how often Uncle Rupert beat me. 'He looks as if he's
got a good swing to his arm,' he said. Not wishing to seem
impertinent, I managed to laugh it off, without saying that
Uncle Rupert would not hurt a fly, let alone beat one. Not
even with a rolled-up copy of the Church of England news-
paper. And, many years later, at a cocktail party, I overheard
two portly businessmen agreeing that the loss of regular ritual
beating was the ruin of the educational system. I really believe
they meant it.

Corporal punishment, of course, has been a deeply in-
grained practice in English boarding schools, reluctant to die,
and of questionable motivation. Certain well-known members of staff at Housey were known to practise it somewhat
above the call of duty, and even the house monitors were
allowed to administer a fairly harmless slap on the behind

with their uniform girdles. Again, it was not always used for the purpose intended. There was one house monitor upon whom I had a crush, and I rather think it was mutual. He is long dead now, killed in North Africa, and was much mourned in the house, for he was very popular. When he was on dormitory duty in the summer term (I must have been just twelve) I would make a point of being illegally out of bed – a beating offence – when he came on his rounds to check on us.

He had flaming red hair and freckles, and he would beat me with his bare hand through my pyjamas. It was fairly innocent, and we both enjoyed it, but I wonder now whether this was the kind of thing Mr Grantully was remembering.

While I was ashore in Aden my most prized possession had disappeared. It was an album of pictures, rather like cigarette cards, which I had collected from five-cent bars of Cadbury's milk chocolate. I had managed to buy these largely from the proceeds of the sale of all those bottles at Owombo, and I had collected all but about five of the cards. Kings and queens of England, British trees, cricketers, and similar generic titles – I had learnt a great deal from my collection and was very proud of it, and now it was gone. I assumed that, as my trunk had no lock on it, the culprit must have been some little Arab who had swarmed up the side of the ship and climbed in through the porthole. But nothing else had been taken: all my clothes, my stamps and my books were exactly as I had left them. Perhaps jocular little Mr Tompkins had another passion, besides Eno's Fruit Salts. I was never to know.

The blow of this loss was softened by the fact, as I have

already mentioned, that I now had a friend. She was the violinist in the ship's orchestra. As the ship's orchestra only consisted of a piano, a cello and a violin, she was quite a personage on board. The players were three sisters from New Zealand, in their thirties – Pat, Doris and Bridget – and Bridget was my friend. I think their name was Sturdee. She was not beautiful, but pleasant-looking, with a good figure. Doris, the youngest, was mousy, gentle and shy, and played the cello. Pat, the pianist, was the eldest of the three, and the leader. She was tall and plain and rather forbidding.

It was Bridget who had given me the good advice. I had been trying to eat something in the dining room. The sea was not so choppy, and I was more or less all right if I kept my eyes on the deck. But if I looked up, the rise and fall of the horizon still set my insides into reverse. I was taking the shortest possible route back to the relative security of my cabin when this lady stopped me.

'Feeling seedy?' A thin New Zealand accent. I nodded. It was all I dared to do, with my teeth firmly clenched over my restless breakfast. She took my arm and led me firmly over to the rail. 'You should stay in the fresh air,' she said. I leant dizzily over the sea. The air was not very fresh, and there was not much of it. The sun was very hot. I looked at the horizon. I was brimming with nausea.

'Now take some deep breaths.'

I did as I was told, and gradually realized that I was not going to be sick; in fact, I began to feel distinctly better. I found I could look at waves with interest.

After a while, we began to talk. She told me always to come up on deck if I began to feel sick. I looked at her gratefully.

'You play in the band.'

'Orchestra.' She corrected me, and laughed. She said she had seen me on my own, and where were my parents? Her eyes opened wide when I told her that I was alone. She told me about her home in New Zealand, about mountains and Maoris and flightless birds. I told her about Mr Tompkins and the Eno's, and made her laugh. I found that I was not minding about the motion of the ship, and we saw some flying fish. I was enjoying myself.

After dinner that evening (which I ate with gusto) we walked together round the whole length of the deck till she had to go and play her violin for after-dinner coffee and dancing in the saloon. I followed her, and she smiled at me over her bow. Pat caught her look and gave me a cold stare as she automatically strummed out the newest fox-trot.

I couldn't wait to get to breakfast the next morning, to see if my new friend was there. She was, and so were her two sisters. Doris, the cellist, was friendly in a dim sort of way. Pat was brisk and impersonal. Not unfriendly, just cool. She was not going to have her conversation broken into by any ten-year-old, however deprived. Bridget smiled widely, and made room for me at their table. I was uncertain, but the stewards, smart and attentive in their tuxedos, hurried to lay a place for me.

'This is your place now,' Bridget said. Pat gave an unconfirming look, and went on with what she was saying, but I was adoringly grateful, and tucked into an enormous breakfast, seasickness forgotten. I did not even mind that they had to go to the saloon to practise a new piece of music. Bridget had said, 'See you later?', with that peculiar upward inflection characteristic of New Zealanders. (I did have a moment of anxiety before the trip ashore at Aden, in case she thought I did not want to be with her, but I doubt if she had even noticed that I had gone.)

She was sympathetic about the loss of my album, and filled my cup of happiness by saying that when we reached Port Sudan she and her sisters were going to take a trip over the coral in a glass-bottomed boat, and would I like to come too? I took no notice of Pat's 'You don't have to come if you don't want to,' and accepted with alacrity. My life was transformed. Every day, there was something to look forward to, now that I had found my sea legs and a friend. That night we walked the deck again – just the two of us. I chattered my head off; it was my first chance to talk since leaving home. I made her laugh, too, which was very heady. All of a sudden the ship had become my home.

Mr Tompkins left the ship at Port Sudan. I never found out what he did, though I am sure he told me, for he was a garrulous little man. But I seldom listened to him properly; he was not my friend, somehow. This was bad of me, because he had been kind and helpful when I was so sick and sad. But the Eno's had become something of a threat, and I also found him a bit embarrassing. We parted amid a lot of advice about washing behind my ears, and making sure that I did my duty every morning after breakfast. As a leaving gift, he bequeathed me his bottle of you-know-what. All this I scarcely noticed. I was going ashore with Bridget; everything else was pale and boring in comparison. So Mr Tompkins – commercial traveller, schoolmaster, petty thief? – went out of my life, and I had the cabin to myself.

Port Sudan. Hot and noisy, full of touts and beggars, and the exotic – and other – smells of the Levant. I stared around in happy bewilderment and clung tight to Bridget's hand. We found the man with his special boat, and set off excitedly, sitting round the large glass central bottom plate, staring into the murky green water and the bubbles streaming past. I was beside Bridget and she did not seem to mind that I sat very close. Actually there was an awning to keep the fierce sun off us, and a coolish breeze off the water, so I had a sort of excuse. Doris was on my other side, friendly and spinsterish. Pat was her usual distant self, and I sometimes caught her looking at us speculatively, but I was used to her by now and was not bothered by it.

The coral and the fish were spectacular, and we pointed things out to each other with ooohs and aaahs. Sometimes our hands touched. Accidentally, I suppose. We ended the trip arm in arm.

The Suez Canal is a kind of single-track road with passing places, and it was weird to look out of the porthole and see a camel undulating disdainfully past only a few feet away. At one of the passing places an enormous ship was parked to let us by. It seemed to have tier upon tier of decks crowded with cheerful men in sand-coloured uniforms waving down to us. I

241

asked Bridget who they were. Italians, she said: soldiers on the way to Abyssinia. Why? There is a war there, she said. Were they friendly? Well – so far . . . I stared at them as they waved and whistled, and I heard my father's voice: 'If there's a war, you won't see me for dust.' I did not understand why that merry shipload suddenly seemed menacing.

It was early November when we entered the Mediterranean and the nights began to get cooler – cooler, at any rate, than the desert. One night I waited in the saloon till the orchestra had swooped out the last waltz of the evening, and when Bridget and I walked out onto the deck it was quite dark, with phosphorescent lights dancing in the water. A breeze had sprung up and I was chilly through my tropical clothes. Bridget was wearing a fur coat and after a while, as we walked the deck, she remarked that I was shivering. She opened her coat and wrapped it round both of us. I put my arm tentatively round her waist, and was not rebuffed. I knew that an African girl like Namuhorsi would not have been surprised if I had made a grab for her breast, but instinctively I felt this was different. But I did want to. There was a reserve about me, and for once I was tongue-tied. Perhaps she had not noticed, for she talked cheerfully enough, and I felt warm and safe. When I went to bed that night I was happier than I had been since leaving home.

The night we passed Stromboli, spouting gouts of red-hot lava into the dark sky, Bridget and I stood at the rail inside her fur coat, with our arms round each other. At one point she kissed me and I swam off into heaven. Some time later, with the volcano not much more than a red glow astern, Pat came and found us, and said rather disapprovingly that it was time I was in bed, and began talking music plans to her sister. Bridget pushed me away gently, and said quietly, 'I'll come and say goodnight.' I went obediently to my cabin, full of happiness, tumbled into bed, and was almost immediately asleep.

The next morning at breakfast Bridget's face went sort of soft round the edges when I said good morning, and sometimes she needed to be asked more than once to pass the toast. I was surprised at her absent-mindedness – she was usually so bright at breakfast – and Pat gave her an occasional look, part pitying, part irritated. The atmosphere was odd.

After breakfast, when she could get me alone, she took my arm and we walked out on the familiar deck.

'You said some lovely things to me last night.'

'Did I? What?'

'Don't you remember?'

I didn't, but some instinct told me not to say so. I just smiled.

'Lovely things. I hope you meant them . . .'

What had I said? I did not know what she was talking about. When had I said these lovely things?

'Um . . .'

'You know – when I came to say goodnight to you.'

'Oh . . . Yes . . .' I had no memory of her coming to say goodnight, except a hazy recollection of her face near my pillow as I lay on the top bunk. I must have talked in my sleep.

Her face was all tender, and her lips parted. She had a kind of beauty, and my heart gave a flip. But what on earth had I *said*?

'I hope you meant them,' she said again.

'Of course I did.' I would have done, too, I was sure, but I wished I had been awake, to remember. It must have been something pretty precocious, from the look on her face. Oh, Simiu – what did you teach me?

With great persistence people in England kept trying to talk to me about the facts of life. Facts which I had absorbed like a puppy from my little black friends. I am sure dear Mr Willink had a go, though I cannot recall it, except for a faint memory of his Adam's apple working double-time in his earnestness. My housemaster, the Reverend 'Boggy' Johns (his initials were WCS) gave me a rather perfunctory and factual account during my confirmation classes, and I remember being rather astonished by the apparently cool impassivity of the actions he was describing. A prep-school headmaster showed me a few simplistic diagrams once, and Aunt Ailie surprisingly chose one morning before breakfast to summon me to her bed to explain about the bees and the flowers. At least, that must have been her intention, but when I answered her question, 'Do you know how babies are born?' by saying, but with embarrassment, 'Well – erm – the man clambers on top of the woman—' She said quickly, 'Yes, well, I think breakfast must be ready. Up you get.' And that was about it. But my knowledge, though graphic and mechanically fairly accurate, was a long time maturing to anything like what it ought to have been and, like most people, I learnt by trial and error. But that is a different story . . .

That night, Bridget kissed me goodnight on the lips. I had no idea how to respond, but I liked it, and supposed I was in love. All the same, when she wrapped her fur coat around us both, I still did not dare to touch her breast . . .

By the time we reached Genoa I had taken to wearing two shirts, because it was getting chilly, and I had no vests, and the fur coat worked overtime. We came to Genoa after dark, and the lights riding up the hills behind were exceedingly beautiful. The city in daylight hardly lived up to them. By this time Bridget and I were inseparable, and the other two sisters treated us with weary resignation. When they were working I spent as much time as I could listening to them. I suppose they were pretty middling, but I thought they were wonderful, and knew their somewhat downmarket repertoire by heart. 'Rose Marie', 'Tea for Two', 'Red Sails in the Sunset' and all the latest Coward, Irving Berlin and Ivor Novello numbers. One tune followed another in my head as if it was all one piece of music – with, of course, suitable intervals for applause. Bridget, tidy on the violin; Doris, swoopy and swimmy on the cello; and Pat keeping them strictly in time on the piano. I loved them all – or thought I did – because they were in Bridget's orbit.

We went ashore at Marseille, just Bridget and I. The other two did not want to – they had seen it all before. Bridget thought I ought to see the mariner's church, high up above the town. It was getting on for mid-November by now, and I was wearing two pairs of underpants as well. I had my first experience of chapped thighs. Bridget was very tender and lent me a scarf to wear round my neck. It did not do a thing for my thighs, but it smelt of her, so I loved it.

We took the hideously steep funicular railway up to the church, and halfway up a couple of English voices could be heard saying what dodgy engineers the French were. I looked down what seemed like hundreds of feet of sheer railway line, and Bridget put her arms round me and made soothing noises. I would not have minded then if French engineering lived up to its reputation. It didn't, and the view from the top was sensational.

She kissed me before we came down and told me not to be frightened. It did the trick. I wasn't.

It became very rough in the Golfe de Lyon, choppy and uncomfortable, but, thanks to Bridget's advice, I rather enjoyed it, and was not as frightened as I expected to be. Then suddenly it became calm and sunny as we passed the Balearic Islands. I was basking alone on the deck, and overheard two of the sailors talking about the Spanish Civil War which was raging on the mainland at the time. They were outdoing each other in their reports of the dangers and cruelties that were going on, especially about the indiscriminate bombing. At that moment a small biplane flew over, and began swooping down over the ship, the Spanish markings plain to see, and I could swear I saw the guns poking out from the wings.

'I'm going in. Hope he doesn't decide to have a go at us,' one of the sailors laughed, and stepped smartly out of the line of fire.

I cowered under a lifeboat, petrified with terror, thinking of those cheering Italian soldiers and waiting for the machine-guns to start stuttering. When they did not, and the plane finally zoomed away, I crept out from my lifeboat and hoped no-one had seen me. It seemed even more unbelievable that Father actually wanted to go to war. 'You won't see me for dust,' he had said. Insane.

According to my father, the Bay of Biscay was a pig, and ships were lucky to get through it. This reputation has stayed with me all my life, and the threat of *the bay* loomed over a lot of the voyage for me. Our visit to Gibraltar was overshadowed by it. Even so, we climbed the Rock, held hands while we fed the apes, and had our breath suitably taken away by the huge rainwater catchment place, which screamed down part of the steepest side.

Actually, *the bay* was rather a disappointment. Very calm, foggy and cold, as was our passage up the Channel. Our mood matched the weather. I was getting nervous as to what to expect when we reached London, and I suppose Bridget was gloomy that our idyllic voyage was coming to an end. I could not give her an address in England because I did not know it, and she never volunteered to give me hers. Even our regular tramps round the deck were restrained. There were long silences, I seem to remember, and we spent a lot of time clinging to each other as we walked. It got quite uncomfortable sometimes, but I did not want to break the spell.

The English Channel was rather eerie – oily still water, cold, thick fog, and the monotonous boom of foghorns. I was hating the thought of our parting, but mixed with it was excitement and nervousness at what was in store when we landed. Bridget was very quiet and, once, I realized she had been crying. She would not tell me why.

At last we turned the corner into the Thames estuary, and could just make out the flat, dreary shoreline through the murk. We anchored for a while before the estuary narrowed and the traffic became crowded. When Bridget came to say goodnight we were both aware that it was the last time. We were very restrained; the fun had gone, somehow.

In fact, it was the last time we spoke. Some time in the early hours the engines had started thumping away, but when I woke early, all was quiet. We had docked during the night. I dressed up in my full gear – hat and all – and went up on deck. It was bright, but freezing, and the deck rails were slippery with frost – a new and not very pleasant experience, for I had no gloves. There was a lot of activity, and already people were leaving the ship. I knew that Auntie Duff (whom I did not know) was going to meet me, but I had received a message that she could not be at the dock till after ten o'clock. I was free to look for Bridget to say goodbye, but there was no sign of her in our usual places. The Petries, and others whom I had got to know, left with a lot of hearty waving. But no Bridget. I was so cold, even with two shirts and two pairs of underpants

248

and my overcoat, that I went below and dug out an extra pair of trousers before my luggage was taken away, and put them on. It was a tight fit.

I arrived on deck in time to see the three Sturdee sisters walking down the gangway. Pat was in front, striding purposefully off the ship. Doris was bringing up the rear in her usual fluttery way, waving to someone on deck. And Bridget was in the middle, with her head down, and a handkerchief clutched in her free hand. I called out, twice, but nobody took any notice.

I called once more, and I saw Bridget stop. Immediately her sisters took her arms and made her walk on. She never looked up, though I know she heard my call. The three of them disappeared into the customs shed. I thought of running after them. But, supposing my aunt arrived and could not find me? She would probably just go away again, and I would be left alone on this freezing ship for ever. I never saw Bridget again.

The time crept up to ten, and still no Duff. By now, all the other passengers had been met, and had left the ship in little laughing groups. The deck was empty, except for a few sailors going about their business. I was dying for a pee, but dare not leave the deck, in case my people arrived and went away without finding me. I had a little weep, but that only made my need to pee worse. I began to get desperate. The time was ten-thirty.

Eventually, I could bear it no longer. I dashed below to the loo, but with two pairs of shorts as well as two pairs of pants, my exit route was far from straightforward.

I had just managed to free myself, and begin my longed for

relief, when a steward rushed in and said my family were waiting for me. By now I was so scared they would leave without me that I quickly started to put away what little I had in that icy place, with predictably moist results. Did my flies up on quite the wrong buttons, and tore back on deck, where sweet, poppy-eyed Aunt Edith was waiting apologetically. Her driver had taken wrong turnings in unfamiliar streets and got lost. I knew it was her. I had seen photographs. She seemed nice.

I took one more look down to the dockside. It was almost entirely deserted.

We had whiting with their tails in their mouths in the restaurant in D. H. Evans, and Duff told the waitress proudly that I was her nephew just landed from Africa, and the waitress was suitably impressed. I felt stiff in my new clothes, and my vest tickled. I had never worn one before. Or a flat tweed cap. Or those woollen gloves. But I was warm – nearly. And, after our visit to Westminster Hall and a cup of tea in an ABC, we made our way to Euston and the train home.

Did any of this really happen as I have described it? The memory of witnesses who give evidence in court is notoriously unreliable. They have only had to think back a couple of months. This story took place, some of it, over sixty years ago.

But one thing I remember as if it were yesterday. As that train clattered along through the November murk, Duff lit her cigarette to give herself courage, and took a deep breath: 'We're not going to Leamington,' she said.